职场交际英语

English in Workplace Communication

刘 菲 王 譞 禹 杭 姜雪华 崔孝彬 编

对外经济贸易大学出版社

中国·北京

图书在版编目（CIP）数据

职场交际英语 / 刘菲等编. —北京：对外经济贸
易大学出版社，2023.6

ISBN 978-7-5663-2532-7

Ⅰ．①职… Ⅱ．①刘… Ⅲ．①英语–口语–高等学校
–教材 Ⅳ．①H319.32

中国国家版本馆 CIP 数据核字（2023）第 149008 号

职场交际英语
English in Workplace Communication

刘 菲 王 瓛 禹 杭 姜雪华 崔孝彬 编

责任编辑：杨娇娇

出版发行：对外经济贸易大学出版社	邮政编码：100029
社 址：北京市朝阳区惠新东街 10 号	邮购电话：010 – 64492338
网 址：www.uibep.com	发行部电话：010 – 64492342
资源网址：www.uibepresources.com	E-mail：uibep@126.com

成品尺寸：185mm×260mm	印 刷：北京时代华都印刷有限公司
印 张：9.25	版 次：2023 年 6 月北京第 1 版
字 数：186 千字	印 次：2023 年 6 月第 1 次印刷
ISBN 978-7-5663-2532-7	定 价：38.00 元

前　言
Foreword

　　本教材以习近平新时代中国特色社会主义思想为指导纲领编写而成，旨在全面贯彻党的二十大精神和教育方针，坚持教材建设国家事权的基本遵循，坚持正确的政治方向、舆论导向和价值取向，落实立德树人根本任务，培养新时代"德才兼备"的外语人才。本教材力图帮助学生坚定"四个自信"，提高学生语言能力、思辨能力和跨文化交际能力，成为有家国情怀、有全球视野、有专业本领的社会主义建设者和接班人。本教材注重培养学生的综合交际能力，使学生能在未来职业相关的业务活动中顺畅地用英语进行口语交流。

　　本教材面向非英语专业研究生或英语专业高年级本科生，也可供已经进入职场或即将进入职场的人士使用，作为提高职场英语语言交际能力的参考书使用。本教材以内容依托式教学法（Content-based Instruction，CBI）为理论指导，沟通交际为主要视角，强调语言系统与内容的整合。本教材将常见的职场情景和常用的商务知识相结合，由书面交际和口语交际两个部分组成。教材在编写过程中以典型职场交际情景为主题模块，划分成 10 章。1—5 章以书面交际为主，聚焦职场招聘、初入职场，主要介绍职场交际中需要的书面交际知识，涉及招聘广告阅读与撰写、英文简历和求职信的撰写、职场面试指导以及职场常用公文的撰写（例如 e-mail）；6—9 章以口语交际为主，内容包含产品展示（口头报告）、职场社交、电话交际和会议交际四个单元。本教材以常见的职场交际礼仪收尾（第 10 章），旨在帮助学生更好地了解职场文化和规范，从而增强交际自信。

　　本教材特色鲜明：

　　（1）贴近职场需求，设置内容模块。本教材的主题选择和内容编排上尽可能还原真实职场场景，从职场的方方面面帮助学生更好地了解职场，掌握职场中必备的知识、语言和交际技能。

　　（2）取材真实，实用性强。本教材的范文及输入材料基本源于真实的国际职场素材，力求让学生在感受原汁原味英语的同时了解职场的真实情况。

1

（3）目标清晰，编排科学。本教材编排以话题为单元。每一个单元章节教学目标清晰。内容紧扣主题和教学目标，层次分明，逻辑清楚，可读性强。

（4）突显人文性，做到人文性和工具性和谐统一。本教材以交际性为目的，集"知识性""技能性""专业性"和"人文性"为一体。注重学生的语言素养、知识素养、思维素养、文化素养和实践素养的同步提升。内容包含对职场所需的专业知识、语言知识、中外职场文化差异和交际策略的讲解以及练习实践，强调对学生职场基本知识技能的掌握和在该情景下对英语语言应用能力及有效得体交际能力的培养。

本教材在编写过程中参考了国内外相关网站和其他相关资料，同时也得到了西北工业大学研究生院、对外经济贸易大学出版社及诸多同仁的大力帮助和支持。彭瑞琪、蓝敏今、李亚丰三位硕士研究生对本文稿进行了多次核对，在此表示衷心的感谢。

《职场交际英语》是本团队在研究生课程改革中的一次大胆尝试。鉴于时间仓促，水平有限，疏漏和不妥之处在所难免，敬请各位专家、学者指正。

编　者
2023 年 3 月

目 录

Contents

Part I Written communication at workplace

Chapter 1 Job advertisements and application letters ················ **3**

Section 1 Job advertisements writing ················ 3

Section 2 Application letter writing ················ 5

Chapter 2 Writing a CV/resume ················ **11**

Section 1 British CV vs. American resume: What is the difference? ················ 11

Section 2 General resume formatting guidelines ················ 13

Section 3 Resume basics ················ 15

Chapter 3 Cover letters ················ **21**

Section 1 Basic structure of a cover letter: key elements ················ 21

Section 2 Cover letter tips: expert advice for graduates ················ 25

Section 3 Cover letter samples ················ 26

Section 4 Useful expressions for cover letters ················ 28

Chapter 4 Job interviews ················ **31**

Section 1 Types of job interviews ················ 31

Section 2 Common interview questions ················ 33

Section 3 Non-verbal communication etiquette in interview ················ 40

Chapter 5 Workplace writing ················ **43**

Section 1 E-mail writing ················ 43

Section 2 Memo writing ················ 54

Section 3 Meeting minutes ················ 57

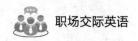
职场交际英语

Part II Oral communication at work

Chapter 6 Presenting a product or service ···················· **65**

Section 1 Introducing products in a presentation ···················65

Section 2 Essential phrases on how to present a product or service···················73

Chapter 7 Business socializing ···················· **77**

Section 1 Workplace greetings and introductions···················77

Section 2 Making small talk at the workplace with colleagues and coworkers········91

Section 3 Business visits ···················98

Chapter 8 Telephone communication···················· **103**

Section 1 Business telephone procedures ··················· 103

Section 2 Making phone calls ··················· 106

Section 3 Telephoning strategies ··················· 116

Chapter 9 Business meetings ···················· **121**

Section 1 Basics of business meetings ··················· 121

Section 2 English phrases for a workplace meeting ··················· 123

Section 3 Rules of a good meeting··················· 129

Chapter 10 Workplace communication etiquette and office culture ··········· **133**

Section 1 Basic rules for communication at workplace··················· 133

Section 2 Workplace etiquette ··················· 135

Section 3 Work culture around the world ··················· 137

Part I
Written communication at workplace

Chapter 1

Job advertisements and application letters

An effective job advertisement for recruiters can target and attract potentially suitable candidates and fend off the others. An effective application letter can help job seekers stand out in the competitive job market by pushing their application to the top of the stack and help them win an interview.

 Learning Objectives

> Identify the key elements of an effective job announcement/application letter
> Develop the basic skills of writing a job advertisement/application letter
> Explain the importance of job advertising in recruitment

Section 1   Job advertisements writing

1. What you need to know about job advertisements

A job advertisement (ad in short) is also known as a job announcement, employment ad, hiring ad, recruitment ad, or a job posting. It is an announcement of a job opening, aiming at informing potential applicants of a new opening and attracting them to apply. Written in an engaging tone, it contains information not only about the job vacancy, but also about the company of recruitment and the benefits it offers. A job advertisement might appear on a company's bulletin board, website, or blog; or in print media, such as newspapers, magazines, and industry-related publications; or on career sites, job boards, and social networking sites.

2. Job advertisement samples

Read the following two job advertisements and summarize the key elements of an

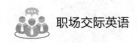

effective job advertisement.

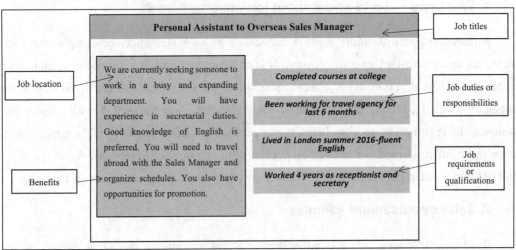

3. Writing an effective job advertisement

➢ Job title. Keep it clear, accurate, and to the point. Avoid unconventional and vague job titles.

➢ Job location. This is one of the main criteria job seekers use in job search.

➢ Job responsibilities. Keep it simple and mention only a few key duties and responsibilities.

➢ Job requirements. List qualifications related to education, working experience, technical and soft skills.

➢ Pay and benefits. Include information about salary range, exciting projects, and benefits.

➢ Applying instructions. Explain clearly who, how and when an interested candidate should contact.

Section 2   Application letter writing

1. What you need to know about application letters

A job application letter or a cover letter should be sent as an introduction for your resume when applying for a job. It is submitted to your potential employer to express your interest in an open position and would help you get the attention of the hiring manager or recruiter responsible for reviewing applications. It intends to convince them why they should offer you an interview if it is well written. It should be noted that an application letter should not repeat your resume, but complement it with a snapshot of your best skills and talents in a concise one-page format. An impressive application letter would distinguish you from the other applicants.

2. Tips for writing an effective application letter

➢ Customize your application letter. Do not use the same application letter to every job position you will apply for.

➢ Show your sincerity in writing. Do not make your application letter emotionless.

➢ Refer to the job advertisement. Do not repeat your resume; instead, highlight your most relevant skills, experiences, and abilities.

3. Structure of effective application letters

When writing an application letter for a job, follow the steps below to make sure you

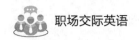

include information about yourself and your professional experience that will appeal to a hiring manager.

> Open the letter by describing your interest.
> Outline your experience and qualifications. You need to focus on those closely related to the job position. You can also tell the reader which of your experiences, qualifications, or abilities would make you an asset to the company.
> Include aspects of your personality if needed.

 **Sample**

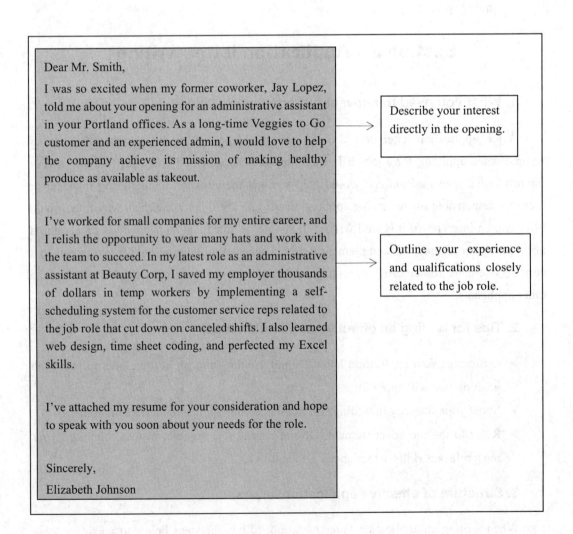

Dear Mr. Smith,

I was so excited when my former coworker, Jay Lopez, told me about your opening for an administrative assistant in your Portland offices. As a long-time Veggies to Go customer and an experienced admin, I would love to help the company achieve its mission of making healthy produce as available as takeout.

Describe your interest directly in the opening.

I've worked for small companies for my entire career, and I relish the opportunity to wear many hats and work with the team to succeed. In my latest role as an administrative assistant at Beauty Corp, I saved my employer thousands of dollars in temp workers by implementing a self-scheduling system for the customer service reps related to the job role that cut down on canceled shifts. I also learned web design, time sheet coding, and perfected my Excel skills.

Outline your experience and qualifications closely related to the job role.

I've attached my resume for your consideration and hope to speak with you soon about your needs for the role.

Sincerely,

Elizabeth Johnson

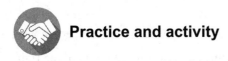 **Practice and activity**

1. Read the following passage discussing the importance of job advertising in recruitment and think about the effectiveness of job advertisements that you once read.

Finding the right candidate can now take little effort and even less time. This is because job advertisements are engaging, brief, and to the point, which could answer the fine points of the job. Although the main goal is attracting potential candidates, job advertising does a lot more than just that. From aiding in your day-to-day recruitment process to enhancing your employer's brand value, job advertising is an all-encompassing solution. To know more, here are some reasons why job advertising is important in expanding a company's digital reach.

Rule No.1 Let the word out

Advertising plays an important role in getting people to know about your job openings. With a lack of proper advertising, your open position might receive little response. For this, it is always a good idea to post your job on various job boards to target a large pool of candidates. The more job boards you advertise, the better your chances of attracting more candidates.

Since job boards are viewed by a large number of candidates every day, it will maximize your reach. Thus, the probability of the open position getting filled sooner also increases. In addition to this, you can also promote your job openings on the best social networking sites.

Rule No. 2 Accessible to everyone across the globe

Posting on various job boards and social media platforms ensures that your ad remains active and accessible 24/7, unless you decide to take it down. Further, it can be viewed by any potential candidate from across the globe. This is especially beneficial for candidates looking for a job remotely. Not only can you post the job without spending an extra minute in your office, but the candidate can access it from the comfort of their homes.

Rule No. 3 Make your company known

In addition to attracting potential candidates, you also make your company known to a larger audience through job advertisements. So, your company and the kind of work it does will be known to a larger audience which will ultimately help them recommend you to like-minded people. The presentation of your company culture on the job ad will help people identify your company values. In addition, you are likely to get more engagement in your job post and on social media channels.

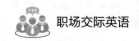

Rule No. 4 Help you filter the right candidates

Mentioning the job role and the skills required would automatically exclude people who do not meet the defined criteria. It could save both the time and effort in filtering out the right candidates.

Targeted job advertising can reduce the number of junk resumes you receive. Therefore, the recruitment processes a lot more efficiently with less frustration. You can also add a questionnaire to your job ad to help you filter applicants in the initial stages.

Rule No. 5 Give you access to a larger talent pool

Job advertising targets job seekers across the web, helping you generate a pool of qualified candidates in your database. Depending on the job requirements, you can contact the job candidates that fit the profile. Further, having access to a larger list lets you engage with passive candidates via recruitment advertising and filter them for later requirements.

Rule No. 6 Make the application process smoother

Apart from stating the job requirements and company details, your job ad can also mention the application steps or include a direct link to your website, making it a no-sweat solution for the candidates. All that the candidate has to do is log in with his/her credentials, fill in the details, upload his/her resume, and apply instantly. Not only can they apply on the go, but you can track all the applications with ease. This means that you can now manage the application process without having to read through a hundred e-mails.

Rule No. 7 It is free (most of the time)

Most job advertising software offers free trials or charges a nominal fee for job postings. All you have to do is sign up and get access to a list of different job description templates. Pick the one that matches your post requirement, make alterations (if any), and you are good to go. To save time, you can filter your search by job title and customize the template to match the tone of your company. All in all, job boards are affordable compared to tying up with a physical recruiting agency.

2. Design a job advertisement for your dream company. Exchange your designed job advertisement with your partner and write an application letter for the job offered by your partner.

3. You are planning to start your own business after graduation. However, your parents believe it is not an opportune moment yet. You have read the report to the 20th

National Congress of the Communist Party of China which says the government will "improve the system for creating jobs by encouraging business startups and support and regulate the development of new forms of employment". Thus, you are very confident about being self-employed. How will you persuade your parents to support you?

 **References**

BARRETTO W. What Is the Importance of Job Advertising in Recruitment? [EB/OL]. 2020-11-24. https://www.jobsoid.com/what-is-the-importance-of-job-advertising-in-recruitment/.

Chapter 2

Writing a CV/resume

Your CV/resume (also written as résumé) is the first opportunity to make a good impression on a potential employer. A high-quality CV will considerably boost your chance of getting a face-to-face interview, so it is worth spending time and effort on the content and presentation. It will make all the difference in obtaining the position you want. Therefore, you should highlight your skills, expertise, and value.

 Learning Objectives

➢ Develop basic skills to write a CV & resume
➢ Expand vocabulary related to CV & resume
➢ Cultivate the awareness of cultural differences in writing a CV and resume

Section 1   British CV vs. American resume:

What is the difference?

In British English, the document that you use to apply for a job is called a CV. It stands for "curriculum vitae", which in Latin means "(the) course of (my) life". While in American English, this document is called a resume, which is basically French for "a summary".

1. What is a resume?

● **In the US:**
A resume (it is fine to leave out the accented é in both American and British English) is

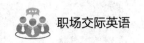

the preferred method of applying for a job in the US. It is a concise document designed to make you stand out from the competition. It is kept short, typically only one page long, for the ease of employers. Because of its restricted length, the information you give on your resume, detailing your education, employment history, skills, and achievements, needs to be kept relevant to the position you are applying for.

This means that a resume is highly tailored, and job seekers in the US will usually rework their resume for every position they apply for. Additionally, it doesn't have to contain information in chronological order, nor does it have to cover your whole career.

Longer resumes are sometimes asked for in the US, typically for more technical roles, and within the academic world, and here the employer would indicate that they would like to see a "professional resume" rather than a "short resume."

- **In the UK and some Commonwealth countries:**

Resumes are rarely used; in Britain the preferred format is the CV, which is slightly longer and includes more details.

2. What is a CV?

- **In the US:**

In case that the word CV is used in the US, it tends to be restricted to academia and university CVs. In America, a CV is generally far longer than a resume (think of 10 pages instead of one or two) and contains a list of all of an applicant's achievements, publications, awards, responsibilities, etc. It is not commonly called for when applying for nontechnical or academic roles.

- **In the UK:**

Traditionally, a CV is an in-depth document that gives an overview of a person's entire career, in chronological order, spanning several pages. It includes details of your academic grades, where you went to school, and other accomplishments, like awards and honors. It also typically includes a small personal statement, detailing your aims, (objectives) hobbies, and interests outside of your career.

It is designed to give a complete picture of your "course of life" and is supposed to be static, that is the same CV is used regardless of the job you apply for and you make changes only to your cover letter, not your CV.

Today, however, a CV in the UK tends to fall somewhere between a traditional CV and a resume. As a general rule, employers don't want to have to read pages and pages about every single one of your achievements. So CVs nowadays have been slimmed down, typically about two pages, detailing only your achievement(s) that are relevant to the specific job you are applying for.

Everything is still listed in chronological order, and some details about your education are given—although high school details tend to be omitted in favor of higher education only, i.e., forget your school grades, but do include details of your university or college course(s) and grades.

Yet, British CVs are now tailored for each different job you apply for.

3. Which variant to use?

A resume is preferred in the US and also in Canada. Americans and Canadians would only use a CV when they were applying for a job abroad, or if they were looking for an academic or research-oriented position.

A CV is preferred not only in the UK, but also in countries that have much in common with the UK, such as Ireland, Australia, and New Zealand.

Section 2   General resume formatting guidelines

The goal of a resume is to tell the story of your experiences as they relate to a specific job description. A great resume can capture the attention of a recruiter or hiring manager and help you stand out from other applicants. When designing your resume, you can remember the following tips:

➢ Color: Stick to the basic black-and-white resume.

➢ Page: Keep your resume to one page. Save it as a PDF or print it on resume page.

➢ Font: Use a simple, classic font like Times New Roman or Arial. Typically 12 pint Times or 10-point Arial is easy for most people to read when printed.

➢ Margins: Keep your margins between 0.5 and 1 inch for the top, bottom, left and right.

➢ Tense: Use past tense in describing past positions and use present tense for your current position(s).

1. Types of resume formats

The three most common resume formats are chronological, functional and combination resume. When deciding which resume format you should use, consider your professional history and the job you're applying for.

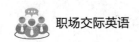
(a) Chronological resume

A chronological resume lists your experiences in reverse chronological order. This is the most popular resume format, especially for job seekers with lots of relevant experience. It is used when:

➢ You want to emphasize advancement to progressive levels of responsibility.

➢ You want to illustrate a stable work history.

➢ Your current job is in the same field as the position for which you are applying.

➢ You are applying for a job in a conservative field or industry.

➢ Your potential employer is likely to prefer a more traditional looking resume.

A chronological resume format usually includes the information in the following order:

➢ Contact information

➢ Objective or summary statement

➢ Relevant skills

➢ Professional experience

➢ Education

➢ Additional information (i.e., volunteer work and special interests—optional)

(b) Functional resume

A functional resume is organized around your skills and abilities rather than your work history. It helps you downplay your lack of experience in a particular field. It is used when:

➢ You want to emphasize specific skills that are closely related to your objective.

➢ You are making a career change and you want to illustrate how skills acquired in one setting can be transferred to a new field.

➢ Your recent work experience is unrelated to your current job objective.

In some cases, a functional resume might be too limiting. If you have some experience and few or no gaps in your employment history, a combination resume might be the right choice.

A functional resume format usually includes the following information in this order:

➢ Contact information

➢ Objective or summary statement

➢ Summary of relevant skills

➢ Work experience

➢ Education

➢ Additional information (i.e., volunteer work and special interests)

(c) Combination resume

A combination resume format emphasizes skills and accomplishments, recent work history, and it is a good choice if you are a junior or mid-level candidate with relevant skills that match the job description. It is used when:

➢ You are an early career professional with 1–3 years of job experience.

➢ You are a recent college or high school graduate with minimal work experience.

➢ You are changing careers or industries.

➢ You have worked with only a few employers but have a consistent work history.

➢ You have no gaps in your work history.

Sections in the combination resume format usually follow this order:

➢ **Name and contact information.** Regardless of format, your resume should begin with your name and contact information so employers can easily get in touch.

➢ **Summary.** Your resume should include a brief summary that quickly promotes your most relevant skills and experiences. And it shouldn't be too long.

➢ **Skills and abilities.** Following the summary, include your skills section. You should list both hard (technical) skills as well as soft (interpersonal) skills.

➢ **Professional experience.** If you are using a combination resume, your professional experience should help support your skills section.

➢ **Education.** Educational history and experience vary in importance based on your professional experience. Adding this section may help to supplement resumes with little professional experience.

Section 3　Resume basics

The resume is the most important tool in the job-seeking arsenal. A good resume can help you get your foot in the door, while a poor resume will likely keep you from even being considered.

1. Basic rules

Rule No. 1 Use fragmented sentences to get to the point

➢ Don't write your resume in the first person.

➢ Drop the word "I" and re-write your sentences.

Rule No. 2 Mind the voice and tense in your resume

➢ Keep the voice of the resume consistent.

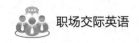

> ➤ Write everything in the past tense.

Bad example:
I answer phones at a call center and sell products to customers. My weekly goal is $10,000. I usually sell about 5% over goal each week.

Good example:
● Responded to over 75-inbound sales calls daily. ● Regularly exceeded $10k weekly sales goal by 5% or higher.

Rule No. 3 Start your statements with powerful action verbs and bullet them

> ➤ Action verbs can help you transform your resume from a simple list of job duties to a dynamic picture of your achievements and abilities.
> ➤ Bullet points can make your statements clear and readable.

LEADERSHIP	
Led	Led and coached 10 employees at four sites across the country.
Directed	Directed operations for over 20 associates in a 30,000 square foot warehouse.
Expanded	Expanded operations from a 12-person organization to a workforce of 56 employees.
Organized	Organized seven leadership conferences and three annual conventions.
Instructed	Instructed a team of 9 associates from diverse backgrounds.
Awarded	Awarded with commendation for "Best Performance Of The Year" among 200 associates.

Rule No. 4 Apply the following principles

> ➤ Use numbers to make your resume more specific and impressive to hiring managers.
> ➤ Showcase your accomplishments, work experience, skills, etc. relevant to the position you are applying for.

Bad example:
I am a construction manager. I supervise a group of employees who build new homes.

Good example:
● Managed construction of new luxury homes. ● Led a team of 29 employees.

2. Tips for writing the education section

The education section will showcase:

➢ Your college name and time of graduation as well as your major.

➢ Your academic achievements, extracurricular activities, special projects and courses.

Further information you need to know:

➢ Your major is put after your college name and time of graduation.

➢ The expected degree awarding date is presented if you have not graduated yet.

➢ Your GPA (Grade Point Average) can be listed below the major only if it is impressive.

3. Tips for writing the experience section

The experience section is a record of your work history. It can provide vital information for hiring managers to make a quick decision about your credentials. Your experience will catch the eyes of hiring managers when you focus on your work's outcomes in particular accomplishments. The following three tips can help you write the experience section.

➢ Ditch the job description. Do not present your day-to-day responsibilities.

➢ Emphasize your accomplishments. Hiring managers are more interested in your potential value.

➢ Quantify the outcomes of your work. Numbers, dollars and percentages will jazz up your experience.

Bad example:
Significantly increased revenues and grew client base between 2018 and 2019.

Good example:
Increased revenues from $250,000 in 2018–to $1.5million in 2019 and tripled client base from 2,500 to 7,000.

 Practice and activity

Please read the following resume example and write your own CV/resume.

Gillian Jones
24 Beech Road, Blaby, Leicester LE87GX
Mobile: 0776324716
E-mail: g.jones@leics.ac.uk

Career Objective
Forward-thinking and confident media graduate with well-honed communication skills and proven ability to build relationships, seeking an entry-level position in public relations.

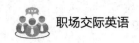
Education

2008-2011   2:1 class BA Communications, Media and Society, University of Leicester
Relevant modules include: Advertising Culture and Communication, Media Audiences, The Media in Britain, Media, identity and the Popular, New Media and the Wired World, Analyzing Communication Processes

2004-2008   Trinity Upper School, Nottingham
A Levels—English(A), Sociology(A), Psychology(B)
GCSEs—11 GCSEs, grades A+—C including English and Mathematics

Relevant Work Experience

Summer 2010   **Internship**, Hopwood PR Agency, Leicester
- Tasked with writing press releases, speaking to journalists by telephone, organizing photo shoots.
- Managed Agency's Facebook and Twitter accounts and posted content on the website blog.
- Supported Agency Deputy Director in a project on behalf of a national client to help produce publicity materials and initiate a social media campaign.
- Gained insight into what skills are needed to establish a successful PR career by talking to staff.

2009-2010   **Features Writer**, The Ripple, University of Leicester
- Conducted research for articles and wrote pieces to reflect some of the typical issues and concerns facing students at university.
- Carried out proof-reading and presented ideas to the editorial team for forthcoming editions.
- Required effective time management skills in order to meet tight deadlines.

Additional Work Experience

2010-2011   **Bar Staff**, The Watering Hole, Leicester
- Popular drinking venue within central city location, constantly interacting with customers during peak periods.
- Entrusted with responsibility of cashing up not long after starting employment, making sure that the tills balanced and takings were correct.
- Demonstrated capability to work in a fast-paced environment faced with competing demands.

2008-2010   **Sales Adviser**, K Shoes, Nottingham
- Worked as part of a team to help achieve set monthly targets which consistently delivered on earning our team best sales team in regional area.
- Advised and assisted customers, recommended products and new stock, maintaining a friendly yet efficient service.
- Took charge of running of shop floor and supervising other junior sales assistants, delegating tasks when shop manager was redeployed to other stores.

 References

CAWLEY CAREER EDUCATION CENTER. Resume Formatting [EB/OL]. 2023-08-16. https://careercenter.georgetown.edu/major-career-guides/resumes-cover-letters/resume-format ting-tips/.

HERNANDEZ G. How to Write a Resume in 2023 [EB/OL]. 2023-04-06. https://www. livecareer.com/resources/resumes/how-to/write/8-simple-steps.

INDEED EDITORIAL TEAM. Combination Resume Tips and Examples[EB/OL]. 2023-06-28. https://www.indeed.com/career-advice/resumes-cover-letters/combination-resume-tips-and-examples.

Live Career [EB/OL]. 2013-08-16. https://www.livecareer.com/resume.

The Muse [EB/OL]. [2023-08-16]. https://www.themuse.com/advice/resumes.

WILL. BRITISH CVS VS AMERICAN CVS—WHAT'S THE DIFFERENCE? [EB/OL]. 2023-08-16. https://englishlive.ef.com/blog/career-english/british-cvs-vs-american-cvs-whats-the- difference/.

Chapter 3

Cover letters

A cover letter (or covering letter) is a one-page business letter, between 250 and 500 words, where you further explain your background, skills and interest in a potential new job. What you put in your cover letter should complement the information in your resume and give the employer a glimpse into your personality. The first thing a potential employer sees in your job application is the cover letter. This doesn't just support your CV—it's an opportunity for you to stand out from the crowd and persuade the recruiter to put you through to the next round.

 Learning Objectives

➢ Develop basic skills to write cover letters
➢ Expand vocabulary related to cover letters
➢ Identify cultural differences and similarities between writing a CV and resume

Section 1 Basic structure of a cover letter:

key elements

The cover letter tips below summarize what should be in a cover letter and the proper order it should follow:

1. Header

The header of a cover letter contains both the contact information and the employer's

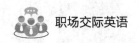

contact information.

- **Contact information**

Start with your contact details and then include the date you send the cover letter. Make sure the contact information in the cover letter heading is accurate and professional (no silly e-mail addresses like big-fish-99@qq.com here). Write your contact information under your name in the cover letter header—as you would in your resume. This includes:

➢ First and last name

➢ Professional e-mail address

➢ Phone number

➢ City and state where you reside

➢ Optional: LinkedIn or relevant social media handles, portfolio or website link

- **Employer's contact information**

Take the time to research the receiver's address in the cover letter (such as a team manager). Knowing how to address a cover letter correctly is crucial because you don't want it to end up in the wrong hands. If you can't find the hiring manager's name and are not sure how to address a cover letter without a name, just address the letter to the department. For example, "Dear Accounting Department."

Below your contact information and left-aligned, write the date and the company's contact details, including:

➢ First and last name of the hiring manager, or the person you're writing to

➢ Company address

➢ Company phone number

➢ Hiring manager's e-mail address

2. Greeting

With the contact details done, here is how to start a cover letter in the right way. Avoid a generic salutation, such as "To whom it may concern"—it's outdated, unless you are uncertain about the receiver's information. Use titles if needed (e.g., "Dr."), and standard honorifics ("Ms." instead of "Mrs.").

3. Opening paragraph

Write a cover letter that communicates what makes you unique, and why you believe you're the right person for the job. Keep your tone enthusiastic and present a specific example of your skills or work history as a "hook" to grab the employer's attention. Just take a look at the example below and you'll see how to write a good opening paragraph for a cover letter that immediately catches your reader's attention.

4. Body paragraph

What should a cover letter include in the body paragraphs? In your cover letter writing, talk about your best professional qualifications, your unique skills and how you can contribute to the company's success. Explain what you like about the company and why you want to work with them. Here's how to make a cover letter stand out:

➢ **Provide further details on work accomplishments.** If you can throw in quantifiable achievements in your cover letter writing, do so. Numbers are great indicators of impact and they help hiring managers get a better grasp of your abilities.

➢ **Explain what has motivated you to change careers or jobs and how your skills will contribute to the company.** Make a cover letter that highlights transferable skills—it's a great way to show the employer that you have the capacity for the job.

➢ **Draw a connection between your past experiences and how they can be applied to the potential job.** This is particularly helpful if you're returning to the workforce after a pause or changing careers. What should a cover letter do to accomplish this? It's simple! Just connect your previous job responsibilities with what the new job requires. Don't have work experience? No problem! Connect this new opportunity with a personal project, extracurricular activity or internship.

➢ **Show your knowledge of the company and the job you're seeking.** Hiring managers know when you did your research. Write a cover letter that shows you understand their culture, goals and environment. This will help you convey that you're the best candidate for the role and a good fit for the team.

5. Closing paragraph

If you've ever wondered how to write a good cover letter closing paragraph, it's pretty easy. Conclude your cover letter with a round-up of your strengths, reiterate your interest in the job, and most importantly, provide a call for action by giving the employer incentive to get in touch with you. You should also encourage the recipient to follow up (e.g., "I look forward to further discussing my qualifications with you.").

6. Closing salutation

What should a cover letter say at the end? Wrap up your cover letter with a professional

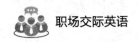

sign-off, followed by your full name. The most common is "Sincerely," but you can also use "Best regards," and "Thank you."

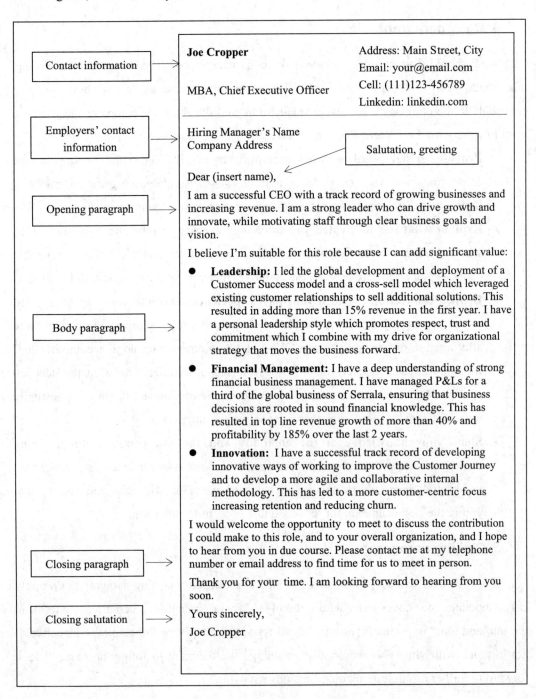

Joe Cropper

MBA, Chief Executive Officer

Address: Main Street, City
Email: your@email.com
Cell: (111)123-456789
Linkedin: linkedin.com

Contact information →

Employers' contact information →

Hiring Manager's Name
Company Address

Salutation, greeting

Dear (insert name),

Opening paragraph →

I am a successful CEO with a track record of growing businesses and increasing revenue. I am a strong leader who can drive growth and innovate, while motivating staff through clear business goals and vision.

I believe I'm suitable for this role because I can add significant value:

Body paragraph →

- **Leadership:** I led the global development and deployment of a Customer Success model and a cross-sell model which leveraged existing customer relationships to sell additional solutions. This resulted in adding more than 15% revenue in the first year. I have a personal leadership style which promotes respect, trust and commitment which I combine with my drive for organizational strategy that moves the business forward.

- **Financial Management:** I have a deep understanding of strong financial business management. I have managed P&Ls for a third of the global business of Serrala, ensuring that business decisions are rooted in sound financial knowledge. This has resulted in top line revenue growth of more than 40% and profitability by 185% over the last 2 years.

- **Innovation:** I have a successful track record of developing innovative ways of working to improve the Customer Journey and to develop a more agile and collaborative internal methodology. This has led to a more customer-centric focus increasing retention and reducing churn.

Closing paragraph →

I would welcome the opportunity to meet to discuss the contribution I could make to this role, and to your overall organization, and I hope to hear from you in due course. Please contact me at my telephone number or email address to find time for us to meet in person.

Thank you for your time. I am looking forward to hearing from you soon.

Closing salutation →

Yours sincerely,

Joe Cropper

Section 2　Cover letter tips: expert advice
for graduates

We asked a panel of career advisers how graduates can ensure their cover letter survives an employer's cursory glance and spells out why they are perfect for them:

1. Draw out all the reasons you're suitable for the job and wave them under the employer's nose.

It's not uncommon for graduates to worry that referring in a cover letter to experience and achievements mentioned on the CV will be repetitive and unnecessary as the recruiter will get to the CV eventually. The result can be a letter with bland, unsupported statements creating a distinctly underwhelming first impression that is anything but a good advert for the CV. A good cover letter should whet the employer's appetite to read your CV—and ultimately to meet you—by drawing their attention to your experiences and achievements which most convincingly showcase your skills and suitability for the role.

2. Think of your cover letter as a love letter, setting out why you and the employer are perfect for each other.

Make sure it is relevant to whom you are writing to and what you are writing for. Generic cover letters do not work as they do not focus and give concrete examples, or enable a prospective employer to see how you fit with them. One professional HR actually suggested to me that students and graduates should approach employers with a cover letter that reads like a love letter. He meant that you should be writing and telling them why you are for them and why they are for you—why you are the perfect match. If you are applying for a specific role, make sure that you look at their criteria and match this to your skills and experience, giving examples of where you have developed these skills. Your examples can include previous employment, course projects, volunteering, etc. The way you present your cover letter will make a big difference in whether it is read or not.

3. If a letter reads well, looks and feels good, then it is likely that the recruiter will identify those qualities with the candidate.

Consider providing a follow-up opportunity or action "I will telephone you on the

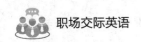

morning of..." or "I am available for an interview..." Keep your letter clear and concise—preferably on one side of plain A4 paper. Remember KISS (keep it short and simple). And finally, use quality paper and a high quality printer. If a letter reads well, looks and feels good, then it is likely that the recruiter will identify those qualities with the candidate. A good cover letter will not get you a job alone, but it might encourage an employer to single out your application in preference to others.

4. An uninspiring cover letter increases the risk of your CV not being read.

Your cover letter is the packaging for your CV, just as the design of a bottle represents the perfume inside or the picture on a box represents the chocolates it contains. You need to take care that your letter is consistent with the style, presentation, and quality of your CV, and makes the employer want to open the packaging to find out more about you. Sadly, many people underestimate both the importance of the cover letter and the skill involved in writing a good one; this increases the risk that the employer never reads your CV at all.

5. It is essential that you tailor your cover letter to the organization you're applying for.

A generic letter you send out to any company advertising a suitable vacancy will not get you anywhere except the bin. It is really worth doing your research and devoting a paragraph of your letter to why you want that job in that company. It's very easy these days to find out information about any organization by doing your research on the internet. See if the company has a mission statement or an operational strategy. If it runs a graduate scheme, try to find out what the current trainees say about their jobs. There are usually quotes on the website. Don't regurgitate what you read in your letter as that will be spotted immediately, but you can pick out salient points so that the employer knows that you have taken the time to find out what they do in more detail. Make sure you mention the name of the company at least once and, if relevant, say something about the location of the job and why that is important to you. Employers will not be impressed by your level of research.

Section 3　Cover letter samples

Standard, conservative/formal style: This is ideal for sectors such as business, law, accountancy and retail. For more creative sectors, a letter like this might be less appealing, and could work against you.

Dear Mr. Black,

Please find enclosed my CV in application for the post advertised in the Guardian on 30 November.

The nature of my degree course has prepared me for this position. It involved a great deal of independent research, requiring initiative, self-motivation and a wide range of skills. For one course, [insert course], an understanding of the [insert sector] industry was essential. I found this subject very stimulating.

I am a fast and accurate writer, with a keen eye for detail and I should be very grateful for the opportunity to progress to market reporting. I am able to take on the responsibility of this position immediately, and have the enthusiasm and determination to ensure that I make a success of it.

Thank you for taking the time to consider this application and I look forward to hearing from you in the near future.

Yours sincerely

Standard speculative cover letter: It refers to a letter sent to a specific company telling them you're interested in working with them and enquiring whether there are any job openings that match your skills and experience. This may vary according to the nature of the organization and the industry you're applying to.

Dear Mr. Brown,

I am writing to enquire if you have any vacancies in your company. I enclose my CV for your information.

As you can see, I have had extensive vacation work experience in office environments, the retail sector and service industries, giving me varied skills and the ability to work with many different types of people. I believe I could fit easily into your team.

I am a conscientious person who works hard and pays attention to detail. I am flexible, quick to pick up new skills and eager to learn from others. I also have lots of ideas and enthusiasm.

I am keen to work for a company with a great reputation and high profile like [insert company name].

I have excellent references and would be delighted to discuss any possible vacancy with you at your convenience. In case you do not have any suitable openings at the moment, I would be grateful if you would keep my CV on file for any future possibilities.

Yours sincerely

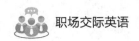

Section 4　Useful expressions for cover letters

1. Opening paragraph

❖ I am writing in response to your advertisement in the Sunday Times, dated 28, April 2012.

❖ Please accept this letter as an expression of my interest in the position of...

❖ A copy of my resume has been enclosed for your review.

❖ I would like to express my interest in the position of...

❖ I am writing to express my interest in the...position at...(company name).

❖ As a recent graduate with...experience, I believe I am a strong candidate for a position at...(company name).

❖ Although I am a recent university graduate, my...(skill) and...(skill) will make me an excellent person.

2. Body paragraph

❖ As seen from my enclosed resume, my experience and accomplishments match the requirements of this position.

❖ I would like to point out...(information relevant to the position)

❖ During my two years with (company name), I initiated extensive improvements that resulted in garnering 30 more clients for the period ending.

❖ I possess the right combination of...skills to be an asset to your organization.

❖ I understand the value of...

❖ I have a very strong interest in...

❖ Experience has taught me how to...

❖ For the past two years I have been working as...at...(company name).

3. Closing paragraph

❖ I would appreciate the opportunity to meet with you to discuss how my qualifications make me ideally suited to the position.

❖ I would appreciate the opportunity to meet and speak with you in person.

❖ I would welcome the opportunity to meet with you to discuss my potential contributions to your company.

❖ I believe that my skill-set perfectly matches your requirements.

❖ I look forward to hearing from you. /I look forward to your response.

❖ If I may, I will contact you next week to discuss.

❖ I would be interested in learning more about...

❖ I look forward to speaking with you about...

❖ Thank you for your time and consideration.

❖ My CV contains additional information on…

❖ It would be an honour to start my career with your company, and I am confident that I will be an asset to the business.

4. Closing salutation

The most common cover letter sign-off is "Sincerely," but you can use the ones mentioned below:

> ❖ Best regards.
> ❖ Kind regards.
> ❖ Thank you.

 Practice and activity

1. Choose the six things you should include in a cover letter. Tick (✓) all the correct answers.

.... Which job you are applying for and how you found out about the vacancy

.... Brief biographical details

.... Your experience and personal qualities related to the job

.... Your negative personal qualities

.... Your motivation for applying

.... Why you left your previous job

.... Your salary expectations

.... A complete list of your exam results and qualifications

.... What you can offer to the company if they give you the job

.... What other documents you are attaching or enclosing with the letter

2. Look at the job advertisements on the website and choose one to apply for. Think about what experience and skills you have that you can highlight. Write your cover letter below.

Scenario 1 Volunteer needed—Daily News

This is a great opportunity for someone interested in a career in journalism. Experiencing writing various types of articles and essays is important, as is the ability to meet deadlines.

Scenario 2 Teaching assistant needed—Hope School

We are recruiting a teaching assistant to help our teachers and students in class. Experience

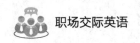

of teaching or looking after children is required. Foreign language skills are desirable.

 ## References

BRITISH COUNCIL. A Cover Letter [EB/OL]. 2023-08-16. https://learnenglishteens. britishcouncil.org/skills/writing/c1-writing/cover-letter.

HANNA K. How to Write a Cover Letter (Cover Letter Tips + Free Templates) [EB/OL]. 2023-03-16. https://www.myperfectresume.com/career-center/cover-letters/how-to/write.

RESUMEWAY. Cover Letter Format: A Step by Step Guide for 2023 [EB/OL]. 2023-01-02. https://www.resumeway.com/blog/cover-letter-format-guide/.

Chapter 4

Job interviews

Making a good impression in a job interview can make the difference between being invited back for a further interview and being rejected immediately by the interviewers. What you say and how you behave can significantly make a deep impression on interviewers.

 Learning Objectives

➢ Understand the differences of various types of interviews
➢ Identify the purposes of interview questions and the moves of answering them
➢ Master the non-verbal communication etiquette in job interviews

Section 1　Types of job interviews

1. Phone screening interviews

Phone screening interviews are calls from your promising employer and are normally performed by one member of the HR department. The call may come at any given time or place without an appointment, aiming at eliminating unfit candidates for the ensuing interviews by asking direct questions. Knowing the following frequently asked questions can help you nail the call.

● **Phone interview tips**
➢ Do your research of the company.
➢ Find a quiet and convenient place.
➢ Cut the distractions.
➢ Mind your tone of voice.

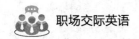

➤ Listen and respond properly.

● **Normal questions in phone interviews**

➤ How did you find this role?

➤ Tell me about yourself.

➤ What do you know about our company?

➤ Why are you the best candidate for the role?

➤ Do you have any questions for me?

2. Video interviews

Video interviews are an increasingly common part of the hiring process especially when you are applying for a remote job. A video interview may take place at or outside of your potential employer's office (in-office vs. remote) and it will be live or prerecorded.

● **Video interview tips**

➤ Ensure that your surroundings are quiet, private and well lit and you will not be interrupted.

➤ Check that your equipment (including webcam, audio, headphone) and internet connection are working smoothly.

➤ Dress professionally—the same way you would for in-person interviews and try to avoid bright colors.

➤ Mind your body language including eye contact, facial expressions, hand gestures and posture.

● **What if things go wrong**

➤ If your video or audio stops working, ask the interviewers for a phone number where you can reach them. Call them at the number if technical difficulties occur to ask if you can continue the interview by phone or if you can reschedule.

➤ If noise interrupts the conversation, apologize for the interruption and ask for a few moments until the noise has subsided. You can mute the microphone for a moment if the noise is severe.

3. Group interviews

Group interviews mean that a number of candidates are interviewed together at the same time. They are typically found for sales roles, internships or other positions in which the company is hiring multiple people for the same job. In a group interview, the interviewers want to see how an interviewee interacts with others, demonstrates his/her skills in a crowd and solves the problems on the spot.

- **Group interview tips**
  - ➢ Show you are unique. It means you need to provide unique examples and accomplishments.
  - ➢ Show you care about teamwork. You need to be polite and friendly with everyone and demonstrate that you are a team player.
  - ➢ Show your personalities. You need to be confident and knowledgeable and demonstrate clarity of thought.
  - ➢ Show you are professional. You need to do your assignment and point out problems and their solutions.

Section 2　Common interview questions

1. Types of interview questions

- **Ice-breaker questions**

Ice-breaker questions are often thought of as "chitchats" which allow both the interviewer and the job candidate to get used to each other. They are simple and rarely include issues of substance but are important nonetheless as they form part of that powerful first impression. Sometimes they could be asked by the receptionist or by someone else who is not part of the formal interview process.

- **Substance questions**

Substance questions are easily recognized by its content as they are about work you have done, the education and training you have received or a qualification you have. They are what the interviewer determines if you are qualified to do the job, as they can be boiled down to the essential of a job interview, "Can you do this job?"

- **Fit questions**

Fit questions can be ice-breaker, preliminary, substance, behavioral or combative. They are asked by the interviewer to figure out if you will be easy to integrate into the company, department, team or what you will be like as an individual contributor.

- **Other questions**

Other questions include too personal questions which are asked by the interviewer to figure out your personality. They sometimes may be those querying your qualification, ability etc.

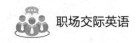
2. Common interview questions and sample answers

Q1: Really cold today, isn't it?

➤ A1: Can't stand it! I wonder if spring will ever come.

➤ A2: Yes, it is. The wind is what really goes right through you.

➤ A3: Yes, it is. We've been so lucky to have had a mild winter; this arctic wind is really a surprise. But I grew up in Minnesota, so it doesn't bother me.

Analysis: The first answer is a strong statement. What if the interviewer is an avid snowboarder? The second answer is much safer as the interviewee does not let on whether he or she loves or hates winter weather. The third answer shows that the interviewee is comfortable with the topic and also adds a bit of personal history.

Q2: Tell me about yourself.

What you need to know

➤ The interviewer wants to know why you are an excellent fit for the job.

➤ You need to prove to the interviewer that you have the skills and experience to be a perfect fit.

Tips for answering this question

➤ Keep the answer short in about two minutes.

➤ Focus on work-related skills and accomplishments, not personal information.

➤ Tell the interviewer why you think your work-related skills and accomplishments would be an asset to the company.

➤ Describe your education or work history very briefly.

➤ Tell the interviewer about things you have done and jobs you have had related to the position you are interviewing for.

➤ Mention one or two personal characteristics that have helped you accomplish your goals, giving short examples to illustrate.

Here is a sample answer

I have always enjoyed working with computers, so it was an easy decision to major in computer science at Tsinghua University with a plan to enter the IT field. In school, I excelled in my computer-related classes and during my college years, I became particularly interested in software development, especially software that would help consumers. That's why I applied for and completed a one-year internship with High-tech Industries.

At High-tech, I learned how to formulate new ideas for software and how to communicate those ideas effectively to the rest of the development team. I am a very focused person and I tend to be product-oriented. At High-tech, I made sure that whatever projects I worked on, I saw to completion. For instance, I worked with a team that was developing a new version of a piece of popular software called Rototype. I asked to be part of every step of software development and at the end of the project, I was given the responsibility of getting final technical approval. I made sure that I followed through with the right departments, keeping my team informed of the progress. This is the type of work I enjoy and that's why I applied for a position with your company.

Your company is a leader in software development and is in the forefront of new ideas in the field. I think that the products your company has developed in the past several years have been outstanding and are the best on the market. I want to work in a company where I can be challenged and where I can make a contribution. I would very much enjoy working in your company to develop new software and to improve existing ones.

Q3: Why do you want to leave your current job? / Why are you looking for a new job?

What you need to know

➢ The interviewer wants to know why you want to work for their company.

➢ You need to minimize any problems and to show that you had positive reasons for leaving.

Tips for answering this question

➢ Never criticize former supervisors, co-workers, or the company/organization.

➢ Don't mention major problems with the management.

➢ Stay positive no matter how bad the situation you are leaving may be.

➢ Avoid sounding like a "job hopper".

➢ Turn this into an opportunity to tell the interviewer about your skills and abilities, if possible.

➢ Keep your explanation short, or the interviewer may think you're making excuses.

➢ Mention positive reasons for leaving.

Sample answer

I've been with High-tech for over five years and I've enjoyed working there. I learned a lot about software development and how to work effectively with my colleagues. About two years ago, I began getting interested in other aspects of design and started learning about new ways that the field is creating and developing new designs. I completed training that qualifies me to oversee other types of projects than the ones I work on now at High-tech. That's why I'm now looking for a company that will allow me to more fully utilize my new skills and where I can take on new challenges. What I see in this position is also the opportunity for growth and advancement. I think that my current skills and abilities are a good match with the current needs of this company.

Q4: Why do you want this job? / Why do you want to work here?

What you need to know

➢ This question gives you an opportunity to show the interviewer what you know about the job and the company.

➢ You need to show that you know a lot about the company and that your qualifications match the company's needs.

Tips for answering this question

➢ Find out all you can about the company, including the department where you would work and the people you would work for.

➢ Research the company's products or services and the positive things it has done for the community or society.

➢ Be familiar with the company's mission statement and core values.

➢ Tell the interviewer how your qualifications meet a need in their company.

➢ Show the interviewer that you are being selective about where you want to work and are not willing to take just any job offered to you.

➢ Don't make the answer all about you. Focus on the positive things about the company, including its reputation in the industry.

Sample answer

This company is an industry leader and is at the forefront of exciting new developments in this field. Its mission to change the way consumers get and send information is, I believe, where the biggest areas of growth are in the industry. Based on the company's financials and its general performance in the past year, High-tech is poised to take over as one of the top suppliers of online service in the world. I have read about the company's many future projects that are designed to move the company forward toward achieving its mission. I want to be part of this company because I believe I can be part of that growth. In the past several years, I have led a number of innovative projects along the same lines as the current direction of this company. By doing this, I was able to help my current company get a foothold in the market. I'm confident that I can bring my proven skills in management, development, and technology to succeed in your organization.

Q5: Why should we hire you?

What you need to know

➢ The interviewer wants to know whether you have all the required qualifications.

➢ You need to be prepared to explain why you're the applicant who should be hired.

Tips for answering this question

➢ Make your response a confident, concise, focused sales pitch that explains what you have to offer and why you should get the job.

➢ Select five to seven of your strengths that correspond closely to the job requirements, and use these as the core for your answer regarding what distinguishes you as a candidate.

Sample answer

> Based on what you've said and from the research I've done, your company is looking for an administrative assistant who is both strong in interpersonal skills and in tech skills. I believe my experience aligns and makes me a great fit. I'm an effective communicator who is skilled in giving oral presentations, speaking on the phone, and communicating via e-mail. I'm also fluent in a number of relevant software programs, including content management systems and spreadsheet suites. I'd love to bring my diverse skill set to your company.

Q6: What is your greatest strength?

What you need to know

➢ The interviewer wants to determine how well you are qualified for the position.

➢ You need to show how your strengths match the needs of the job.

Tips for answering this question

➢ Know the three typical categories of your skills, which are knowledge-based skills, transferable skills and personal traits.

➢ Give specific evidence or examples of how your strengths have helped you in the past.

Sample answer

> One of my biggest strengths is my communication skills. In my current job, I work with people from all over the world and many different backgrounds. I'm able to understand that everyone has different perspectives about projects and work tasks. One of our most recent hires comes from a developing country. It's very tempting when talking about the latest technological developments to dismiss or at least ignore her perspective. However, as the head of the department, it was clear to me that this new employee brought a fresh perspective on why we needed to consider different options when deciding on the type of technology to adopt. Through hard work and determination, I was able to get the rest of the department to make important changes that moved us in the same direction as the project. I was fortunate that I was able to develop these analytical skills when I was an undergraduate student at ABC University. The program I was in used case-based teaching so that we worked on solving real-life problems under real-life conditions. I graduated at the top of my class, and now, I make use of the skills I learned there everyday.

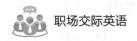

Q7: What is your greatest weakness?

What you need to know

➢ The employer wants to know whether you are qualified to do the job and is also looking for indicators that show you've been able to learn new tasks and handle new challenges.

➢ You need to name weaknesses that can be improved on and that may be an asset in the right circumstances.

Tips for answering this question

➢ Don't try to present a strength as a weakness, such as being a workaholic or being too detail-oriented.

➢ Keep the weakness a small one.

➢ Show how you are working to improve on your weakness and give specific evidence or examples.

➢ Tell the interviewer about a weakness you have already overcome.

➢ Tell the interviewer about a mistake you made in the past to show that you can learn from your mistakes.

➢ Tell the interviewer about a weakness that does not relate to the duties of this job.

Sample answer

A weakness that I have is that I don't like to do public speaking and I get nervous when I have to give a presentation or a speech in front of other people. I realize that I won't need to do any public speaking in this job right now, but I want to overcome this fear so that when the time comes, I'll be prepared. It's important to me to identify any shortcomings that may affect my job performance or career advancement opportunities, and to do something about them.

To combat my fear of public speaking, I took a public speaking class at ABC College a few months ago, and after I finished the course, I joined a Toastmaster club. I have been going to the club meetings regularly where I give speeches in front of other members and I get constructive criticism about my performance. I can say that in the past five months, I have become a better and more confident speaker. I think, however, I can be even better, and that's why I've continued to attend meetings and to look for opportunities to put into practice what I've learned. I'm confident that in a very short time, I'll be an even better and more effective speaker and presenter.

Q8: Describe a difficult work situation or project and how you overcame it.

What you need to know

➢ The employer wants to know how you respond when faced with a difficult decision.

➢ You need to share an example of what you did in a tough situation and details to make the story believable and engaging.

Sample answer

> I think the most difficult situation I face as a production manager is when I have to lay off staff, either because they aren't doing their job properly or, even worse, because sales are down. When I can, I try to work with under-performing personnel to see if we can improve their efficiency. If not, then I hand them their pink slip and give them straightforward reasons for why they are being laid off. No one wants to be fired without an explanation. When this happens, I keep my tone polite and avoid using too many "you" statements; I absolutely do not want to cast shame on them.

Q9: What are your goals for the future? / Where do you see yourself in five years?

What you need to know

➤ The employer wants to know if you're going to stick around or move on as soon as you find a better opportunity.

➤ You need to assure the interviewer that if the company hires you, you will continue working for them, and that you have given careful thought to your future career plans.

Tips for answering this question

➤ Reassure the interviewer that you are not a "job hopper" by telling that you plan to stay and grow with the company.

➤ Research the company to find out the logical next positions to move up in the company.

➤ Show that you are motivated and have definite plans about doing more in the company.

➤ Avoid naming a specific job or position or you will seem too narrow or inflexible.

➤ Do not talk about personal goals or plans.

➤ Questions about marriage, babies, and childcare are illegal, but if you don't plan to make any big personal life changes soon, you can volunteer that information.

Sample answer

> My goal is that in five years, I will be working in a managerial position in this company. I see the next few years here at High-tech Co. as an opportunity to gain the skills and knowledge to run one of the departments in this company. One of the reasons I am applying for this position is that this is a large company with a lot of opportunities for advancement. If I continue working in the department where this position is, I hope to be a senior manager with a hand in shaping the strategic plans for development in this area of technology. Another possibility in five years is to transfer to one of the regional offices, where I would oversee local operations.

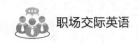

Section 3 Non-verbal communication etiquette in interview

1. Eye contact

● **The importance of eye contact**

➢ Convey confidence. Looking down at your shoes or focusing on the table are actions that can convey a lack of confidence and nervousness. If your eyes in an interview are fidgety or continuously shifting back and forth, this can mean you are trying to conjure up an answer that you are not sure is the right one.

➢ Exhibit honesty. If you've been making great eye contact the whole interview and suddenly start blinking rapidly—more than 70 blinks per minute—when asked a question, this can indicate stress and a desire to avoid the truth.

➢ Show interest. When a candidate is authentically interested in the conversation, there is a chemical released and the eyes dilate. This sparkle, in turn, inspires the employer, letting him or her know your adrenaline is up and you are interested and engaged in what is being presented or expressed.

● **Tips for making eye contact in job interviews**

➢ Make eye contact when you are prepared to answer or ask questions.

➢ Make eye contact but avoid a sudden change in eye contact.

➢ Allow your eyes to light up when the interviewer is talking about something particularly interesting or you are revealing information you are proud of.

➢ If you have more than one interviewer, remember to make eye contact with all of them, not just the person you feel most comfortable with, or the one doing the most talking.

2. Hand gestures

Good and appropriate hand gestures can show your confidence and positive attitude in an interview but there are hand gestures that you should stay away from in job interviews.

➢ Point. Pointing is often perceived as an offensive motion.

➢ Tap or drum fingers. Tapping or drumming fingers expresses impatience, boredom or annoyance.

➢ Rub the back of your neck. Rubbing the back of your neck makes you look uninterested.

➢ Fidget or touch your face. Both transmit a signal of nervousness or uneasiness.

➢ Clasp hands behind the head. Clasping hands behind the head denotes arrogance and superiority.

➢ Cross the arms. Folding arms in front of your chest suggests a closed and defensive attitude. Be in an open gesture with your arms.

3. Handshake

Stick to the following advice to see how to execute the perfect business handshakes.

➢ Get the grip right. Put your hand out, tilt the fingers down and scoop up into the handshake—instead of just sticking your fingers out and letting the other person grab it. The hand's web goes up into the web of the other person's hand, so you get full palm-to-palm contact.

➢ Hold on firmly. Give the person's hand a firm grasp to set the tone that you're confident. Eliminate flimsy, wimpy handshakes from your repertoire and keep them brief and purposeful.

➢ Give it a pump or two. See it as an act unto itself, rather than just something you do to get to the other side of it. As for how long the handshake should last, a few factors come into play—like geography, industry and culture.

 Practice and activity

1. Watch a video about an invitation call of job interview and think about why the caller hung up and what you would do if you were the interviewer.

https://v.qq.com/x/page/b0174sptoyp.html

2. Watch a video about group interview and think about who you will recruit based on their conduct in this interview and why.

https://www.bilibili.com/video/BV1zJ41137zC/?p=2

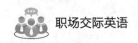

 **References**

FOSTER B. How to Prepare for a Job Interview: Practice Tips to Get Ready [EB/OL]. 2021-03-04. https://www.moneycrashers.com/prepare-job-interview/.

INDEED EDITORIAL TEAM. 7 Tricky Interview Questions with Example Answers [EB/OL]. 2023-06-10. https://www.indeed.com/career-advice/interviewing/tricky-interview-questions#: ~:text=How%20to%20answer%20tricky%20interview%20questions%201%201., process%20...%205%205.%20Maintain%20your%20calm%20.

POWNER T. Types of Job Interviews [EB/OL]. 2023-08-16. https//www.careerthinker.com/interviewing/types-of-interview/.

PAVLOU C. Icebreaker Interview Questions and Answers [EB/OL]. 2023-08-16. https://resources.workable.com/icebreaker-interview-questions.

The Balance Career [EB/OL]. 2013-08-16. https://www.thebalancecareers.com/.

Chapter 5

Workplace writing

Workplace writing is the most common type of writing in workplace. It is directed toward specific results, communicating in ways that are clear, direct, and brief. Workplace writing takes different forms, from formal business letters, meeting minutes, and applications, to brief messages, notes, e-mails, narratives, and added text to letters. In this chapter, widely used workplace writing forms such as e-mails, memos and meeting minutes are introduced.

 Learning Objectives

➢ Familiarize students with the basic structure of workplace writing forms
➢ Equip students with common English expressions used in workplace writing
➢ Teach basic e-mail writing etiquette and rules

Section 1   E-mail writing

E-mail allows companies to efficiently and effectively spread information about their products and services, both to existing customers and potential ones. It is one of the most effective marketing tools as it would be able to reach out many potential customers due to the widely used e-mails. It is important to write e-mails well to avoid misunderstandings, project professional image, enhance credibility and build and maintain relationships. In the business world, e-mails help you communicate with people around the world, transfer files from one place to another rapidly. In order to write effective business e-mails, you, first of all, have to know the e-mail basics.

1. E-mail basics and rules

● **Knowing your audience**

➢ Every time you write something you should have a particular reader or audience in mind. You must adapt the content, tone and language of your e-mail to the situation (context) and intended audience of your communication. This does not only apply to e-mail, but to all forms of communication.

➢ When composing your e-mail, do not assume that the receiver will understand your language. You should always: focus your writing to assist your readers; make sure you know who your reader is before you start to write and take care when using acronyms e.g. TAFE, technical language and even humour.

➢ Appropriateness is the key: pay attention to the appropriateness of language, content and tone.

● **When to use e-mail**

E-mail is quick and easy to use, in particular when you want to:

➢ Provide directional, important and timely information.

➢ Share detailed information and data.

➢ Ensure there's a record of your communication.

➢ Direct the receiver to an online source for more information.

➢ Provide brief status updates.

But sometimes it would be better not to use e-mails when:

➢ Your message is personal or confidential.

➢ The news you have to give is bad. It is easy to sound unconcerned when you deliver unpleasant news by e-mail.

➢ You need an immediate response.

It is very important that you think before you write. Here come some general tips for effective e-mails:

Rule No. 1 Be clear

Use short sentences, simple language and correct grammar.

Rule No. 2 Be brief

You need to keep your e-mails brief by focusing on only one topic, explain your main reason for writing in the first paragraph and be specific about what you want.

Rule No. 3 Write a strong subject line

Your subject line is like a headline in a newspaper. The subject line needs to attract attention and make someone want to read your e-mail. You can write strong headlines by using the "4 U's" approach, i.e. "Unique", "Urgent", "Useful", and "Ultra-specific" (very specific).

Rule No. 4 Be polite

Don't type your message in capitals. Capitals are considered to be SHOUTING and are rude. Be careful with exclamation points! Too many exclamation points will seem like yelling.

Rule No. 5 Create the right tone

Use sentence length, punctuation and polite language to create the right tone.

Rule No. 6 Proofread before sending out

You should always reread your message before you send it and correct any mistakes.

2. Structure of an e-mail

An e-mail is a form of communication. Business e-mails are like letters. As such it has a specific structure. This includes a header, a salutation, an opening sentence, an ending and a closing.

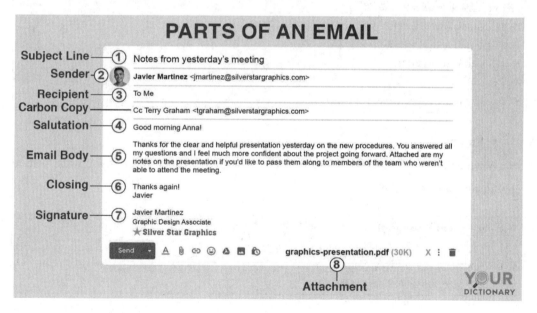

- **Header**

The information contained in the header normally includes the e-mail's sender and recipient(s), as well as the date and time it's sent.

- **Salutation**

The salutation you choose changes depending on who your audience is. It helps set your e-mail's tone. Business greetings often use colons for a professional tone, while exclamation points can make friendly messages familiar and enthusiastic. For example:

❖ Dear Sir or Madam (if you don't know the name of the person reading the e-mail)
❖ Dear Mr. Johnson

Even the word "dear" can feel too formal in a friendly message. Informal salutations immediately establish a casual and friendly tone for the recipient. For instance:

❖ Dear Jim
❖ Hi/Hello, Jim
❖ Hi/Hey/Hello (without name)

● **Opening sentence**

Your opening sentence is the key to writing a clear e-mail. A good opening sentence tells the reader what the e-mail is about. For example, if you're writing to follow up on something, you could start with any of these:

❖ I'm just writing to...
❖ Just a (quick) note...
❖ Just a short note to follow up on...
❖ I'm writing in regard to...
❖ I want to follow up...
❖ I need to bring something to your attention...

● **Ending**

When ending an e-mail, ask yourself what you want the reader to do. If you want them to reply to you, you can write:

❖ I look forward to hearing from you. (formal)
❖ Looking forward to hearing from you. (less formal)
❖ I look forward to your reply. (formal)
❖ Hope to hear from you soon. (informal)

If you want them to contact you when they need more information, you can write:

❖ Do not hesitate to contact me if you need any assistance. (formal)
❖ Let me know if you need anything else. (informal)

If you don't want them to do anything:

❖ Thank you for your help/assistance.
❖ Have a nice day/weekend.

● **Closing**

Your closing will depend on how well you know the reader. Common closings include:

❖ Sincerely (formal)
❖ Kind/Best/Warm regards (less formal)

You may have received e-mails with closings as follows and these closings help create a closer relationship when you already know your reader.

❖ All the best
❖ Best see you (soon)
❖ Take care
❖ Bye (for now)
❖ Have a nice day

3. Writing effective e-mails

As e-mails are short pieces of communication, there is a set structure you should use, which is more like a reversed triangle. Reasons for using this structure are as follows: people are busy and do not have enough time to read everything. The reader will look at the beginning and decide whether to read on. It helps keep the e-mail short and to the point.

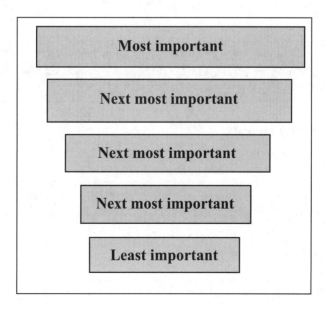

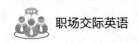

4. Language guide for specific e-mail subjects

In business, people tend to write e-mails to achieve the following purposes:

➢ Clarify something.

➢ Confirm something.

➢ Follow up on something.

➢ Let someone know about something.

➢ Answer a question.

➢ Ask a question.

➢ Thank someone for something.

➢ Update someone.

Here are some English expressions that you can use in different situations:

● **Responding to an inquiry**

If you're writing to reply to an inquiry (a request for information), you need to use the first sentence to let your reader know this is what you're doing. You're also going to create goodwill (friendly and good feelings) with this person who may be your client or customer. For instance:

❖ Thank you for your interest in...
❖ Thanks for choosing...

Here's an example of how you might respond to an inquiry about the cost to install windows in a house:

❖ I'm writing to respond to your inquiry about the cost of installing windows in your house (opening sentence). Please find our price list attached. Do not hesitate to contact me if you need any assistance. Thank you for your interest in ABC Enterprises.

● **Confirming arrangements**

Let your reader(s) know this in the opening sentence:

❖ I'd like to confirm...
❖ Just writing to confirm...

Or you could set a more informal tone by writing:

❖ Tuesday is good for me. (Especially if they have already suggested Tuesday.)

❖ A nice way to end is to write...
❖ Looking forward to seeing/meeting...

- **Informing someone about something**

While what you want to inform the reader of will change from e-mail to e-mail, certain key phrases can help you get your message across clearly. Here are some opening sentences and phrases you can use:

❖ I'd like to inform you of...
❖ I'm writing to tell you about...
❖ Just a note to say...
❖ Just to update you on...

Toward the end of the e-mail, you may want to add:

❖ Hope this helps.

You may also want to offer additional information if needed:

❖ Let me/us know if you need anything else.
❖ Let me know if I can help you further.

- **Changing arrangements**

You've made arrangements and now you have to change them. Any of these sentences and phrases should work:

❖ I'm sorry but I can't do/make Tuesday...
❖ This is to let you know that I've had to put off/postpone...
❖ I'm writing to call off/cancel...
❖ I'm afraid I can't make/manage Wednesday.
❖ How about next Friday instead?

You don't have to go into detail about why you need to change arrangements. The point of your e-mail is simply to change arrangements. Keep it clear and brief.

- **Replying to a previous e-mail**

When you reach out by e-mail to someone you don't know and they write back, the polite thing to do is to thank them for their time. Here's how you can do that:

❖ Thanks/Thank you for e-mail.

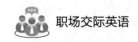

If someone has sent you an e-mail and you write back, you can use one of these phrases at the beginning:

> ❖ In reply to your e-mail, here are...
> ❖ Re: your e-mail, I...

You might have to send attachments. If so, you can write:

> ❖ You will find...attached.

There are times when you might not have all of the necessary information available. Then you might have to make a promise to get back to the sender by writing:

> ❖ I will get back to you ASAP. (ASAP stands for "as soon as possible")

- **Giving good news**

Set the tone for your e-mail right away by telling your reader you're writing with good news. The words "pleased," "happy", and "delighted" work well. Include them in sentences like these:

> ❖ I'm/We're pleased to inform you...
> ❖ I'm happy to tell you...
> ❖ You'll be happy/delighted to hear that...

- **Giving bad news**

Certain words let people know that bad news is coming. I'm talking about words like "regret," "sorry," "afraid" and "unfortunately." Unfortunately (you see I just used one), you'll have to give bad news about business issues from time to time. Here are some opening sentences you can write to tell bad news as nicely as possible:

> ❖ We regret to tell/inform you...
> ❖ I'm sorry, but...
> ❖ I'm afraid that...
> ❖ Unfortunately...

- **Making a complaint**

Complaining can be tough. But it's easier to get what you want if you complain in a way that doesn't offend your reader. The way to do that in an e-mail is not to be too emotional and to make your complaint clear and specific. The following phrases can help you get started:

❖ I'm writing to complain (about...)

❖ I was disappointed to find/hear...

❖ I'm afraid that...

❖ Unfortunately...

- **Making inquiries**

Start by using polite language to request what you want.

❖ I'm interested in receiving/finding out...

❖ I would like to receive...

❖ I would be grateful if...

❖ Could/Can you please send me...?

Are you sure that the person you are writing to can help you? Don't worry if you aren't. Just ask by writing:

❖ Would you be able to (help)...?

❖ Can you help?

If you need an instant answer, don't assume the person you're writing to understands this. Let them know by writing it:

❖ I'd appreciate a reply ASAP.

- **Requesting an action**

There are times when you want someone to do something for you. Here are useful phrases you can use to make your request:

❖ Can you send...to me by Thursday, please?

❖ Please get/keep in touch.

❖ Keep me posted. (Keep in touch)

Note that the word "please" can keep your request from sounding like an order.

5. Basic rules of e-mail etiquette

- **Choose the right e-mail address**

Before actually writing a business e-mail, you have to know first-hand why you are writing and who you are writing to. If you are writing for some workplace matters, use your company professional e-mail address. But if you are writing for a personal meeting, use your

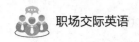

personal e-mail instead.

- **Put the right names in the To/Cc boxes**

To: This area is for your direct recipient, the one whom your e-mail is meant for and you expect their response.

Cc (Carbon copy): This one is for your indirect recipient, you send a copy to inform them so that they acknowledge the content of this e-mail, but they don't need to reply to it. For example, when you are mailing a response to a client's complaint, this part could look like this:

To: A—The client's employee who works with you directly

Cc: B—The client's boss who needs to be informed about this problem

- **Subject**

Never, ever leave a blank subject—this will make people think your e-mail is spam and it would likely end up in their trash box. Keep your e-mail subject clear and direct, short and simple.

- **Opening**

Start your business e-mail with proper opening. Avoid informal words like "Hey" or "Yo" which can make you sound unprofessional. After that, use one or two short sentences to briefly introduce yourself (if this is your first time contacting this person) and mention your reference as well.

- **Body**

Business e-mail structure and notes would be slightly different based on which type of business e-mail you are writing. However, the e-mail etiquette is the same regardless of what kind of content you are writing.

➢ **Keep a neutral, polite tone**

Pay some attention to how you are saying your content: choose formal expressions, use short and sharp, well-written sentences to help your recipient understand your points as clearly as possible without any difficulty. Say "please" and "thank you" when needed.

➢ **Maintain a simple format**

Use simple black text, white background. Choose default fonts (like Arial, Times New Roman, Verdana) so that everybody can read your e-mail, no matter which platform they are using. Use bold, italic, underline when necessary. Don't be creative, don't over-decorate your e-mail or your clients will run away from you right now.

➢ **Provide a call to action at the end**

Conclude your e-mail with a clear call to action that tells your recipient what you want them to do next. You might ask for an in-person meeting, an RSVP, (a reply) a file delivery or a general response. Provide a time frame for this communication, such as the end of the day or the end of the week. This call to action lets your recipients know what they need to do and how much time they have to comply.

> **Include a professional closing**

Conclude your e-mail with a short closing, such as "Thank you," "Best regards" or "Sincerely." Include your full name at the bottom along with your title and essential contact information, such as your phone number.

- **Proofread your e-mail carefully**

Reread your message before sending it. Be sure to check for typos on your own, too. Look for proper punctuation, spelling and grammar. If you're reaching out to an important client, consider having a coworker look over the message as well before sending it on.

- **Respond to messages promptly**

A timely response helps clients and coworkers stay on schedule. A brief response is often appropriate for things like acknowledging receipt of a file or confirming a meeting time.

- **Save your emojis for personal messages**

Though emojis are a common part of popular culture, they're more appropriate for casual messages than business communications.

Examples: The following two sample emails illustrate how inquiries and replies in business are made.

- **Inquiry**

Dear Sir or Madam,
I am writing to ask about your room availability from 16 August to 26 August. Is it possible to book two double rooms in advance?

Looking forward to hearing from you.
Zhang Ying

- **Reply**

Dear Zhang Ying,

I am pleased to receive your email regarding room availability in our hotel.

Plenty rooms are available during that time. We can book two double rooms for you in advance as required. Please tell us your phone number.

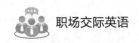

Please feel free to contact us if you have any questions.

Yours faithfully,

Wang Yi

Section 2　Memo writing

A memo (or memorandum, meaning "reminder") is normally used for communicating policies, procedures, or related official business within an organization. It is often written from a one-to-all perspective (like mass communication), broadcasting a message to an audience, rather than a one-on-one, interpersonal communication. At workplace, when you need to update your colleagues on important information or to inform a specific group within a company of an event, action, or observance, a business memo can be an ideal way to address a specific audience in a formal context.

1. The basics of a business memo

While business memos and e-mails may look similar, a memo has some key differences:

➤ More formal than e-mails.

➤ Used when you need to give your message a more official look.

➤ Can be printed and distributed wherever the message would have the most impact.

Memos can be addressed to a single person or a group, so tailor your message to reflect the concerns of your audience. As with any business document, always remain professional and polite, even if you have to address a negative topic. An official memo is no place to single someone out in a critical way, so focus on facts and constructive plans for the future. For the most part, the purpose of writing a memo is to inform. However, memos can occasionally include a call to action or a persuasive element.

Here are some instances when a memo might be useful:

➤ Informing employees about company policy or process changes.

➤ Providing an update on key projects or goals.

➤ Making an announcement about the company, such as an employee promotion or new hire.

➤ Reminding employees about a task that needs to be completed.

➤ Making a request of all employees.

➤ Communicating a message that employees will refer to more than once, such as a detailed proposal or recommendation.

2. Writing a business memo

Like many other professional business documents, memos will include an introduction, body and conclusion.

- **Header**

Start with a header that clearly indicates that the communication is a memorandum, the intended recipients, the sender, the date and the subject.

- **Introduction**

Write an introduction that uses a declarative sentence to announce the main topic of the memo.

- **Body paragraph**

Include a body paragraph with discussion points that elaborate or list the main ideas associated with the memo's topic. To make the memo easier to read, write in short paragraphs and break the information into smaller, more manageable chunks. Since the recipients will likely be scanning the memo, you should also use subheadings and bulleted lists when possible.

- **Conclusion**

Conclude the memo with any remaining information following the body paragraph. This is a summary of the memo and should clearly inform the reader of any actions required. Close with your name, e-mail address and phone number in case anyone needs to contact you. Ensure any necessary attachments are included if your intended recipients will need to refer to other information, such as a graph, image or chart, below the end of your memo.

With simple and effective formatting, a few key tips can be applied to virtually any business document:

- ➤ Use traditional fonts, such as Times New Roman or Arial.
- ➤ Left-align the text.
- ➤ Use single-spaced paragraphs.

Some expressions that can be used:

❖ I look forward to your support in this matter.
❖ We hope that this new policy change will be of greater benefit to our employees.
❖ We are confident that these strategies will lead to a boost in our sales.
❖ I'm excited to discuss your opinions in the next meeting.
❖ Thank you in advance for your continued support.

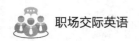

Memo letter template

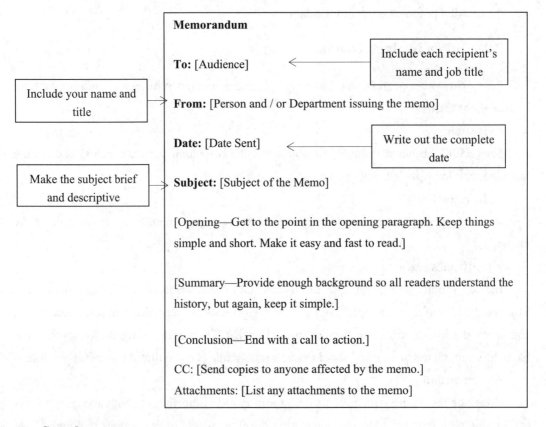

Memorandum

To: [Audience]

From: [Person and / or Department issuing the memo]

Date: [Date Sent]

Subject: [Subject of the Memo]

[Opening—Get to the point in the opening paragraph. Keep things simple and short. Make it easy and fast to read.]

[Summary—Provide enough background so all readers understand the history, but again, keep it simple.]

[Conclusion—End with a call to action.]

CC: [Send copies to anyone affected by the memo.]

Attachments: [List any attachments to the memo]

Include each recipient's name and job title

Include your name and title

Write out the complete date

Make the subject brief and descriptive

Sample memo

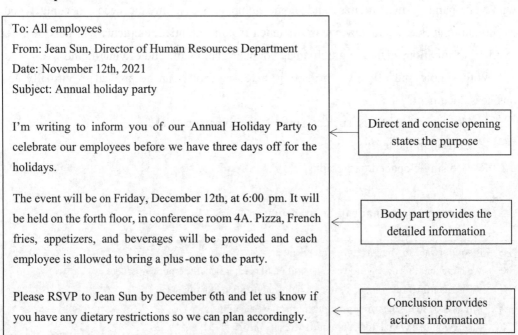

To: All employees
From: Jean Sun, Director of Human Resources Department
Date: November 12th, 2021
Subject: Annual holiday party

I'm writing to inform you of our Annual Holiday Party to celebrate our employees before we have three days off for the holidays.

The event will be on Friday, December 12th, at 6:00 pm. It will be held on the forth floor, in conference room 4A. Pizza, French fries, appetizers, and beverages will be provided and each employee is allowed to bring a plus-one to the party.

Please RSVP to Jean Sun by December 6th and let us know if you have any dietary restrictions so we can plan accordingly.

Direct and concise opening states the purpose

Body part provides the detailed information

Conclusion provides actions information

3. Tips for memo writing

Please keep these rules in your mind as you're writing the memo, to be on the safe side.

➢ **Use bullet points.** If you have several issues to cover in the body, break it up using bullet points. This will keep your memo easy to read and understand quickly.

➢ **Be concise.** Don't include unnecessary details or use tons of adjectives. Keep things simple. Avoid long sentences and wordy phrasing. Make sure that the body of the text is clear, concise and grammatically correct.

➢ **Have a conclusion.** Conclude the memo with any closing statements that may inspire the recipient to take action. Mention any and all attachments at the end of the memo by using the single word "Attachment."

➢ **Do not forget to review.** Even if you're in a hurry, make sure you carefully review and proofread your memo before sending it. We'll provide more in-depth guidance for proofreading later in this post.

➢ **Do not use a salutation.** You should simply go right into the subject of the memo.

➢ **Do not use informal/emotional language.** Keep it strictly formal. No slang words or colloquial language. Even if you're writing about an employee's inadequate performance, don't berate or use sharp words. Be detached but polite in your criticism.

Section 3　Meeting minutes

Meeting minutes, or MOM (for minutes of meeting) can be defined as the written record of everything that's happened during a meeting. They are used to inform people who didn't attend the meeting about the happenings, or to keep track of what was decided during the meeting so that you can revisit it and use it to inform future decisions. This type of meeting notes can actually be written for any kind of meeting that requires an official record. This written record can then be used to inform team members who weren't able to attend and action items that can be revisited. Minutes from previous meetings can therefore be used in order to make future organizational decisions.

1. The purpose of meeting minutes

➢ In some special instances, taking meeting minutes may be required by law, for example during disciplinary meetings with employees or legal disputes. However, in most cases, whether to take notes is entirely up to you. Here's why taking meeting

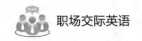

minutes is worth the effort.

➢ Minutes provide a written record of what was agreed at a meeting and create a shared understanding of the outcomes. They are an important source of information allowing participants to reflect on what has happened. A written record is the best way to avoid misunderstandings stemming from people having different recollections of the meeting.

➢ They notify people of tasks assigned to them and create clear timelines to keep everyone on track. They create clarity about what the next steps are and who is responsible for what, making sure no action items are forgotten.

➢ They act as a source of information for members who were unable to attend. They also help other stakeholders stay informed, for example, when the meeting's outcomes impact collaborative, cross-team activities or projects within the company.

➢ They allow participants to go back and revisit the key ideas and discussion points that led to a decision. Without a clear record, it is easy to forget why a certain decision was made. In the worst case, you may end up having to repeat the meeting and have the same discussions all over again.

2. What to include in meeting minutes

The contents of your meeting minutes will depend on your company's needs and the kind(s) of meeting you generally hold. However, the following elements are usually included in most meeting minutes:

● **Meeting basics like name, place, date and time**

It's important to include basic details about your meeting at the top of your meeting minutes. This ensures that everything is organized and that your meeting can be identified at a glance.

● **List of participants, absentees (apologies) or guests (If there is any)**

Include a list of everyone who was present at the meeting. This identifies everyone who is working on or involved with a given project or topic, as well as noting down which employees are informed about what.

● **Meeting purpose**

Every meeting should have one central goal. You might discuss a variety of topics, but there should be at least one main objective on the agenda or sometimes more. It's essential to note this down because it helps provide direction to the meeting and clarity regarding its focus.

- **Agenda items**

Good meeting minutes should include all the agenda items that were addressed at a meeting. If possible, it's a great idea to talk to the meeting leader and note down these agenda items before the meeting begins for maximum note taking efficiency.

- **Date and place for next meeting**

At the end of the meeting, the organizer should determine how long it will be until everyone needs to meet again. Make sure to note down the date and time in your meeting minutes.

- **Relevant documents**

Sometimes there might be additional documents that were discussed throughout the meeting, or you may want to store the document in an easy place so you can refer to it when necessary.

- **Any other business (AOB)**

That is an item on the agenda where members may introduce items such as proposals, motions, questions that are not originally intended to be discussed.

Sample of a meeting minute

Meeting minutes for High-tech Co.

MEETING DETAILS

Meeting Facilitator: John Zhang

Secretary: Mary Ma

Date: November 15, 2021

Time: 10:00 AM

ATTENDEES

Jack Carter, Robert Williamson, Amanda Zhu, Frank Lee, Patricia Smith, Hillary Borgoff.

ABSENCES

Alfred Sun and Michael Landry

REPORTS

- *Financial reports*
  - *Profit and Loss*
  - *Expense Reports*
- *Customer Reviews*
  - *Internal User Feedback*

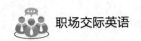

UNFINISHED BUSINESS

● *Updating the Homepage*

➢ *Decide background images*

➢ *Review Design*

NEW BUSINESS

● *New Year Bonuses Amounts ($)*

➢ *Low-level Employees*

OTHER

● *New Years Eve Party*

➢ *Bar Limit($)*

Minutes submitted by: _____   *Print Name: Jessica Smith*

Approved by: _____   *Print Name: John Wu*

---

3. The basics of meeting minutes

● **Take minutes in real time, or make notes after each topic**

Start with the meeting agenda as an outline. Fill in agenda items with more detail while the information is still fresh in your mind.

● **Be concise**

As the minutes taker, your job is to document what is happening at the meeting. But you don't need a verbatim accounting of everything that is said.

● **Only note down the facts**

Avoid personal observations when writing meeting minutes. If you want to take separate notes of your own, you are welcome to do so. But the meeting minutes should be a factual record of what was discussed.

● **Note down the absentees (apologies) who are unable to attend**

With meeting minutes, it's important to write down the names of these who attended the meeting, but also the one(s) who didn't, so there will be no confusion about who may have discussed or voted on an issue.

● **Use a meeting minutes template for the right format**

If you're writing formal meeting minutes, follow a certain format. But with informal meeting minutes, you have more flexibility. Think of what your organization needs, and what's been done in the past. Then improve on that process.

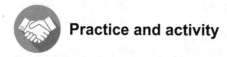

Practice and activity

1. Reading the following e-mail and point out the inappropriateness, then revise it based on the basic rules introduced.

> Subject: Meeting
> Hi Xiaohua
> I just want to remind you of the meeting we have scheduled next week. Do let me know if you have any questions.
> Best,
> Zhong Hua

2. Write a memo for one of the following scenarios. Decide who the memo should be sent to and what the subject of the message is. Add your own information to the body of the memo.

Scenario 1

You are the office manager and want to remind everyone to clean up after meal in the lunchroom. There was recently an infestation of cockroaches. The building has since been fumigated but you still require the cooperation of the staff to prevent a re-infestation. State the purpose of the memo, your reason(s) for sending it (i.e. the kind of behavior you have noticed) and what actions need to be taken.

Scenario 2

Write a short summary of a class lecture in one of your other courses this week. Use a memo to summarize the lecture as if you were preparing it for your classmates who could not attend. Summarize the lecture topic accurately and concisely.

3. Watch a video about a meeting and try to summarize the main task discussed on the meeting and write a minute based on what you have watched.

https://b23.tv/5HMpC2d

References

ALBOUY L. How to Write Meeting Minutes: Ultimate Guide [EB/OL]. 2022-12-20. https://slite.com/learn/meeting-minutes.

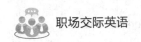职场交际英语

ASHMAN M, CRUTHERS A. Advanced Professional Communication [M]. eCampus Pressbooks, 2021.

CSIZMADIA A. 10 Tips for Effective E-mail Communication [EB/OL]. 2022-12-28. https://www.liveagent.com/blog/10-tips-for-effective-e-mail-communication/.

GROSSMAN D. When to Use Email (and When Not to) [EB/OL]. 2021-09-22. https://www.yourthoughtpartner.com/blog/bid/55776/when-to-use-e-mail-and-when-not-to.

INDEED EDITORIAL TEAM. A Complete Guide to Memo Writing (With Tips and Examples) [EB/OL]. 2023-04-12. https://www.indeed.com/career-advice/career-development/memo-writing-guide.

JOEMILAN, THERING R. How to Write Business English Emails in 8 Steps (Useful Terms and Phrases Included) [EB/OL]. 2023-07-24. https://www.fluentu.com/blog/business-english/business-english-email-writing/.

MAILOSAUR. Structure of an Email [EB/OL]. 2023-08-16. https://mailosaur.com/blog/structure-of-an-email/.

MITTRA A. How to Write a Memo in Business English: 7 Simple Steps [EB/OL]. 2022-04-22. https://www.fluentu.com/blog/business-english/business-english-memo/.

NUCLINO. How to Take Meeting Minutes: Templates & Examples [EB/OL]. 2023-08-16. https://www.nuclino.com/articles/meeting-minutes-template-example.

PUBLISHER A. Business Communication for Success [M]. Minneapolis: University of Minnesota Libraries, 2015.

SITZMAN R. How to Write an Email in English: 18 Office-ready Email Writing Tips (With Sample Emails) [EB/OL]. 2023-06-19. https://www.fluentu.com/blog/english/how-to-write-an-email-in-english/.

TEAM ASANA. How to Write a Memo for Effective Communication (with Template) [EB/OL]. 2022-11-27. https://asana.com/resources/memo-template.

THE HUGO TEAM. How to Write Meeting Minutes [+5 Free Templates] [EB/OL]. 2023-08-16. https://www.hugo.team/blog/meeting-minutes-with-samples-templates#.

Part II
Oral communication at work

Chapter 6

Presenting a product or service

A presentation is not just stating the features of a product but it goes beyond the obvious. With a great presentation, one can educate about the product, provide important information, develop potential customers' understanding and inspire their confidence.

 Learning Objectives

- ➤ To develop basic skills to present a product or service
- ➤ To expand vocabulary related to general business presentation
- ➤ To identify cultural differences between China and other countries in presenting a product or service

Section 1   Introducing products in a presentation

1. A presentation of products

Product presentations often involve prepared statements given by a public speaker, and they might use visual aids like slideshows, photographs or videos. Most product presentations are given by sales associates or specialists who have experience with a certain product, but they can also be given by groups of sales associates or company employees. A product presentation usually contains a few specific elements to ensure that a presenter presents all details about a product to the audience. The major components of a product presentation are Introduction, Agenda, Company information, Positioning, Summary of what you are going to tell the audience, Product description, Benefits, Examples and Closing.

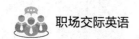
2. How to create a product presentation

Here are some steps you can use to create your own product presentation:

- **Plan your introduction**

Determine how you want to introduce yourself. An introduction in a product presentation can be brief, as it focuses more on the product being described. You can introduce yourself by providing your name, position at the company and your involvement with the product that you're presenting.

- **Prepare your agenda**

Organize the agenda you want to follow during your presentation of products. An agenda is the list of topics you decide to discuss in the order you plan to talk about them. In a product presentation, an agenda can be especially helpful because there is typically a lot of information to cover. Once you determine the topics you want to cover and the order you want to present them in, you can create a visual aid that presents your agenda to your audience.

- **Include information about your company**

Organize some information about the company you work for. Because many customers attend product presentations to learn about new products, they might not always be familiar with the company giving the presentation. Therefore, providing some insight into a company might give potential customers in the audience context for why they're offering a certain product and information about a company's values and missions. To include information about your company, you can use customer lists, funding information, or references to awards or milestones in your presentation.

- **Identify your positioning**

Describe your positioning, or why you're giving this specific product presentation. The positioning can tell an audience about what makes a product unique, why customers should buy it and more. To identify your positioning, you can prepare a few statements that describe attractive or interesting features of a product and explain why it's different than other products in the same market.

- **Describe the product**

Describe the benefits of the product and provide specific examples. This section can tell the audience more about why they might purchase a product by highlighting how it can benefit them. If you know who will be in the audience before you give the presentation, you might focus on discussing benefits that can relate to some particular needs in their lives. You can also use specific examples to show how the product can be successful, which can help an audience picture themselves using a product and relate it to themselves.

- **Provide examples of benefits and success**

Describe the benefits of the product and provide specific examples. This section can tell the audience more about why they might purchase a product by highlighting how it can benefit them. If you know who will be in the audience before you give the presentation, you might focus on discussing benefits that can relate to some particular needs in their lives. You can also use specific examples to show how the product can be successful, which can help an audience picture themselves using a product and relate it to themselves.

- **Write a closing statement**

Draft a closing statement to end your presentation. A closing statement should summarize what you have already talked about in your presentation by briefly referring to your main points. You can also include a call to action that invites customers to ask about the product, give feedback or purchase the product. This can be very effective in encouraging customers to engage with a product or company and retain their interest. At the end of your closing statement, you might leave some time for the audience to ask you questions, which can further inspire participation from the audience.

- **Practice your presentation**

Rehearse your presentation before presenting it to your intended audience. This can help you prepare for the public speaking aspect of a presentation and ensure a clear and complete speech when giving your presentation to customers. To practice your presentation, you can review your materials and speak through your prepared statements out loud to identify places that you might need to practice more. You can practice giving your presentation alone, or you might ask a few coworkers to sit in as a mock audience so you can get used to speaking in front of the audience.

 Practice and activity

The passage given below is about 7 Ways to Introduce a New Product in a Presentation from a business blog. It has seven sections from A to G. Choose the correct way (heading) for each section from the list of headings below.

List of Headings
1. Prioritize Your Audience's Needs
2. Create a Message, Not Just a Product

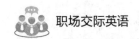

3. Define Your Objective

4. Create a Conversation

5. Say It with Visuals

6. Keep It Simple

7. Communicate with Confidence

Section A:

Like anything, it's always good to start at the beginning, and with a new product presentation the first thing you need to do is to define your objective. Sounds simple, you want people to love your new product, right? But consider more specifically what you want them to do after watching your presentation—should they visit your website, call you, or buy a year's supply of your product?

Whatever it is, define this first and consider your objective in every slide you create, making sure your presentation concludes with a clear call to action.

Section B:

A new product presentation is far from one-size-fits-all and should be completely different depending on who's watching it. Whether you're presenting to investors, retailers, prospects or marketers, put yourself in their shoes and make sure you include everything they need to know. Don't try to include everything for everyone in one presentation, instead create a slide deck for each audience, or use a menu-driven presentation to allow you to present uniquely every time.

Section C:

Millions of products are available today and there are probably even a few out there that are similar to yours. This means that selling a "thing" is no longer enough. It's now essential to have a wider reason for your audience to buy into it.

Explain what kind of journey your product will take people on, share how your business is giving back to society, or explain an interesting or funny story behind the origins of your product. Whatever your message, find it, hone it, and engage your audience by making your presentation a storytelling experience that they enjoy.

Section D:

This is especially important in the time of Coronavirus, when product launches are happening online and you can't get there in front of your audiences. Strong product shots, mock-ups and visualizations will help people to see and understand what you want them to buy into as much as if you were in the room with them.

Section E:

How do you expect someone to believe in your product if it sounds like you don't?

Creating an amazing slide deck that you love will give you the confidence to deliver a brilliant presentation that your audience can believe in.

Section F:

Don't overwhelm people with slides that combine masses of text, multiple images and contrasting fonts. Keep to one point per slide for a much more effective way to connect with your audiences, while minimal on-screen text allows you to flex your muscles on your new product expertise.

Section G:

Avoid "lecturing" audiences and instead turn your presentation into a conversation by allowing people to ask questions, especially while many of us are still working from home, live presentation experiences are great ways to make your presentation interactive. They provide an easy way for your audiences to engage in a direct conversation with you and ensure any questions are answered.

3. FAB approach in main body to convince your audience

The FAB Statements are essential in explaining why someone should buy from you. FAB stands for Features, Advantages, and Benefits. A FAB Statement is explaining the feature, what it does (the advantage), and how that benefits the prospective client.

➢ **Features:** Features are one of the easier things to identify. Highlight the features of the product or service you want the audience to focus on.

➢ **Advantages:** Advantages are what the features do. They show how these features make the product or service better than its predecessors or competitors.

➢ **Benefits:** Benefits answer why someone should value the advantage. They show how this product or service will improve the user's life.

 Practice and activity

1. The conversation given below is by Steven, sales representative for X High-tech Company, who is presenting a new piece of Customer Relationship Management (CRM) software called x Customer.

STEVE:

Well, **good afternoon, ladies and gentlemen**. I'm Steve Dunn and **I want to tell you today about X High-tech Company** new CRM application for your iPhone, the X Customer.

Firstly, I'll demonstrate exactly what this software is capable of doing.

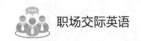

Then, I'll outline the advantages this has over conventional CRM systems.

Finally, I'll show you how this can help boost the productivity of your sales force significantly.

So, first of all, as a salesman I can tell you what we all want is up-to-the-minute information about our customers. X Customer links your salespeople directly with your central customer database so that at any time they can check what exactly the...without any time lost.

Moving on to my next point, what are the advantages of the real-time information provided by X Customer over other CRM systems? Well, it means that for the first time ever your salespeople always have up-to-date details about your customers. Current credit ratings for example, any problems with recent orders or maybe a new special offer that headquarters wants...of course, because it has a phone function."

So, finally, what are the real benefits for your salespeople? Two words: increased productivity. Our research shows that salespeople are able to make at least 15 percent more-customer visits per week, leading to an increased sales volume of up to 30 percent and that's not all. With...

In conclusion, if you commit to using X Customer, we are offering a free consultancy service you're your business. Our experts will visit your company and...

Thank you for listening. If anyone has any questions, I'd be happy to answer them.

CUSTOMER:

Yes, I do. Do you provide software training for users as part of the package?

STEVE:

I'm pleased that you asked that question. We don't provide training ourselves, but our sister company is responsible for that and I'm sure we could discuss ways that we could incorporate into the package.

Please complete the following table with the features, advantages, and benefits of X Customer based on Steve's presentation.

Product	Features	Advantages	Benefits

2. The following are students' FAB drafts on promoting commercial products (e.g. a vacuum cup, a smart phone and an energy vehicle). Read them and discuss with your classmates which product you are most interested in, which product you least like, and what concerns you have if you need to promote and present them.

Student sample 1: The intelligent vacuum cup of Tupperware

Good afternoon, ladies and gentlemen, I'm Tom and I want to tell you about our product, the intelligent vacuum cup of Tupperware.

Firstly, I will demonstrate the outstanding material properties of our product.

Then, I will outline the advantages of this product in terms of intelligence.

Finally, I will show you how healthy this product is.

First of all, the vacuum cup is made of 304 stainless steel and has three layer vacuum processes that keeps water warm for 48 hours. Therefore, you can drink hot water whenever and wherever you want. There are intelligent chips in the cover of the vacuum cup, so it can monitor temperature at all time.

It could display the time and water temperature at any time, and can even be connected to your phone, so you can see the temperature of the water in the cup via your phone APP, thanks to a smart chip on the lid. It can also adjust the water temperature. For example, it can go from 50 degrees to 70 degrees.

Finally, the biggest benefit that our products can give you is health. On the one hand, touching the lid three times can turn on the ultraviolet sterilization function. After tens of thousands of experiments, the sterilization rate of this cup can reach to 99%. On the other hand, the purity of the water can be detected automatically after the glass is turned upside down for 5 seconds. The cup can let you use in happy, and drink at ease.

In conclusion, if you buy this vacuum cup, we will offer after-sale service. As long as exists any quality problem we will offer you a new one. Thank you for your listening, if anyone has any questions, I would be happy to answer you.

Student sample 2: We-Phone

Hello and welcome back to banana park! I'm David and I can't wait to introduce a novel mobile phone—the banana smartphone, we-Phone! Firstly, I'll demonstrate exactly what this phone is capable of doing. Moreover, I'll outline the advantages this has over conventional phone. Finally, I'll show you how the we-Phone can facilitate our life significantly. So, first of all, as a salesman I can show you the powerful we-Phone chip. B14 Bionic is the fastest chip in a smartphone and it pushes what's possible. Like the Holographic Laser Projection. When contacting with others, customers can use it to watch each other in real time with others' permission, just-like face-to-face talking.

Moving on to my next point, the advantages of we-Phone are real and fast. It has the best display, which can provide the most realistic color restoration. Similarly, it has an interesting function. People can charge we-Phone anywhere without using a cable, and it only takes 10 minutes to fully charge it.

Of course, although it has an excellent function, what are the real benefits for you users? Two-key words: efficient and immersive. Our research shows that users are able to increase 15 percent work efficiency than other products, due to B14 Bionic. Also, we-Phone could provide the immersive feeling that users could experience planet viscerally in 3D.

In conclusion, if you decide to buy the we-Phone, we will provide you with the best service. Our sales staff will help you learn how to use this smartphone and understand after-sales information.

Thank you for listening. If anyone has any questions, I'd be happy to answer them.

Student sample 3: New concept driverless energy vehicles

Good evening, ladies and gentlemen. "My name is Liu Kai from group 7. It's my honor to present a product introduction to-you. Our product is "new concept driverless energy vehicles", which aims to ignite a new ecosystem. Here is a video about driverless cars. Below, I will introduce the era "pet" in detail from three aspects of "features", "advantages", and "benefits".

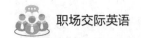

Well, the outstanding feature of the vehicles is the adoption of many high and new technologies. The following points will be explained as follows: First, the car adopts "Beidou navigation technology" to achieve accurate positioning and self-navigation. Second, the car is powered by the latest energy technology, which uses high energy density lithium technology. Third, the car integrates big data and cloud computing technology.

With the support of many high and new technologies, the energy vehicle has the following advantages: firstly, it achieves the highest level of driverless driving (Level 5); secondly, it can achieve quick charging and ultra-long range, with a full range of 2,000 km in 10 min, 2.5 times the range of Tesla; thirdly, clean energy, zero emissions of air pollution, actively respond to the national "carbon peak" and "carbon neutral" policy; Fourth, you can connect everything in the car.

In the end, what does the car really benefits for you? To sum up, the first is freeing your hands without worrying about accidents. The second is super convenience, which can last for a long time on a single charge. The third is to save your money. In the process of use, it is estimated that "one kilometer only needs one dime". The four is freedom, you can do whatever you want, such as drinking, reading even working in the car.

In conclusion, it is not only an electric car, but also an ecosystem for the new era of connected mobility. If you choose the car, we will provide customizable service to meet your personalized needs and free maintenance for life. Finally, we believe that the new concept driverless energy vehicles will run on the land of China in the near future.

Thank you for listening, and if anyone has any questions, I'd be happy to answer them.

Comments and recommendations

Student Sample

What is good about it:

The tone is as welcoming as it is informative. Similarly, much of language strikes a perfect balance between colloquial and technical, and some of the phrasing is quite memorable. Each presentation is structured efficiently and shrewdly. Additionally, rationale is convincing and demonstrates a keen understanding of what audiences are looking for.

What could be improved:

Practice the simplification of verb phrases, the use of the active voice whenever possible, the structure of compound-complex sentences, and the elimination of filler words and phrases that state redundant information. Tightening up each of these areas will reduce unnecessary wordiness and make writing clearer. Additionally, there are a few places that would benefit from increased specificity: think from the audience's perspective and explain anything they might find unfamiliar.

The revised version is as follows:

Student sample 1: The Tupperware intelligent vacuum cup ~~of Tupperware~~

Good afternoon, ladies and gentlemen~~,~~. I'~~'~~m Tom, and I want to tell you about our product, the Tupperware intelligent vacuum cup~~of Tupperware~~.

Firstly, I will demonstrate the product's outstanding material properties ~~of our product~~.

Then, I will outline its ~~the advantages of this product in terms of~~intelligent aspects~~ee~~.

Finally, I will show you the cup's health~~how healthy this product is~~ advantages.

~~First of all,~~Tthe vacuum cup is made of grade 304 stainless steel and~~has~~ features ~~a~~ three-~~-~~layer vacuum process~~es~~ that keeps water warm for up to 48 hours~~,~~. allowing ~~Therefore,you~~can to drink hot water whenever and wherever you want. Additionally, the intelligent chip in the cover ~~There are intelligent chips in the cover of the vacuum cup, so it can~~monitors temperature independently~~at all time~~.

The cup~~It~~~~could~~ displays the time and water temperature at~~any~~ all times~~,~~. ~~and~~ thanks to a smart chip on the lid, it can~~even be~~ connected to your phone,~~so~~ and show you~~can see~~ the temperature~~of the water in the cup via in~~your phone app~~APP,thanks to a smart chip on the lid~~. ~~It~~You can~~also~~ even adjust the ~~water~~ temperature from the app itself. ~~For example, it can go from 50 degrees to 70 degrees.~~

~~Finally,~~Tthe product's~~biggest~~ health benefits~~that our products can give you~~ are ~~is~~its biggest health~~innovation~~. ~~On the one hand,~~Ttouching the lid three times ~~can~~turns on the ultraviolet sterilization function. After tens of thousands of experiments, the manufacturers achieved a sterilization rate~~of this cup can reach to~~ of 99%. The cup detects ~~On the other hand,~~ the purity of the water~~can be detected automatically~~ when it ~~after the glass~~is turned upside down for 5 seconds~~,~~. ~~The cup can~~ letting you~~use in happy, and~~ drink safely and at ease.

I~~In conclusion, if you buy~~ ~~this~~ the Tupperware intelligent vacuum cup now, we will offer you a after~~post~~-sale ~~service~~warranty:~~.~~ ~~As~~ a brand-new replacement for any cups with ~~long as exists any~~ quality problems~~we will offer you a new one~~. Thank you for your listening~~;~~. if anyone has any questions, I would be happy to answer ~~you~~them.

Section 2　Essential phrases on how to present a product or service

- **Welcoming your audience**

❖ Good morning or Good afternoon everyone.

❖ Thank you for coming./Thank you for being here with us today. I would like to welcome you to today's meeting/event.

❖ It's a pleasure to speak to you today.

❖ Ladies and gentlemen, thank you very much for coming along here today.

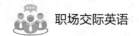

- **Introducing the subject of your presentation**

❖ The topic of today's presentation will be...

❖ I'd like to take this opportunity to walk you through...

❖ My aim for today is that by the end of this presentation each of you will know more about...

❖ The purpose of today's presentation is to discuss how we can...

❖ I've invited you here today to have a look at my findings.

- **Making the structure of your presentation crystal clear**

❖ Today's presentation will take about 30 minutes and will be divided into three key sections.

❖ As time is of the essence. I will only be addressing two of the three key topics today.

❖ I'm planning to cover the following issues.

❖ First of all, I will be discussing... secondly, ... and last of all, ...

❖ Now let me begin by... secondly, ...and finally, ...

- **Making the main points**

❖ I'd like to begin by talking to you about...

❖ Let's kick things off with a quick look at...

❖ Now let's turn our attention to...

❖ I'm conscious of the time, so let's move our focus to...

❖ Next up on the agenda...

❖ Moving on, let's discuss...

- **Coming to a conclusion and ending the presentation**

❖ Seeing as we're almost at the end of today's session, I'll start to wrap up.

❖ That concludes my presentation for today. The main takeaways from today's presentation are...

❖ That's all from me on this.

❖ Thank you for listening./Thank you for your attention.

❖ That's it on ABO advertising for today. In brief, we've covered...

❖ Well, that concludes my presentation today. To refresh your memory, the main takeaways are the following. Number one...

❖ That brings me to the end of my presentation. I hope you're a little clearer on what ABO advertising is and when to use it.

❖ So to draw all that together, next time you think about ABO advertising, consider the following factors...That's all from me!

- **Using visual aids**

❖ If you'd like to turn your attention to the screen, you'll see...

❖ From looking at this graph, you'll notice that... As you can see from the data...

❖ If you look at this graph, you will see...

❖ From this chart, we can understand how...

❖ As you can see from this infographic, our research indicates that...

❖ This chart shows our findings of a recent experiment we undertook. The y-axis represents...while the x-axis stands for...

- **Be ready for questions**

❖ Thank you for that important question, Susan.

❖ That's a great question, and I'm glad you asked it.

❖ That's a challenging question, I haven't considered that before.

❖ You know, that's a tricky one. I'd like to think about it and get back to you on that.

❖ Does that answer your question?

❖ Was that the answer you were looking for? I'd be happy to discuss it more together afterwards.

❖ I'd be happy to invite you to ask questions at the end of the session.

❖ At the end I'd be very happy to answer any of your questions.

 ## Practice and activity

1. The following are phrases for presenting products and services. Match phrases or sentences with those that serve the same purpose.

(1) I want to tell you today about…

(2) Firstly, I'll demonstrate… Then, I'll outline… Lastly, I'll show you…

(3) Moving onto my next points,…

(4) What are the advantages of…

(5) In conclusion,…

(6) If anyone has any questions, I'd be happy to answer them.

(7) I'm pleased you asked that question.

A. First of all, I'll… Next, I'll… And finally, I'll…

B. Let's look now at…

C. My talk today is about…

D. Please feel free to ask questions.

E. To sum up, …

F. That's a good question.

G. Why is this important? Because…

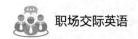
2. Think of a product or service that you would like to promote from your line of work. Complete this table with its features, advantages, and benefits of a product. Then deliver your presentation.

Product	Features	Advantages	Benefits

 **References**

BENJAMINE C. 63 Must-know Business Presentation Phrases to Have Prepared [EB/OL]. 2018-06-15. https://preply.com/en/blog/business-presentation-phrases/.

CLARK K. Features, Advantages, and Benefits (FAB) Statements [EB/OL]. 2012-10- 06. https://devedge-internet-marketing.com/2012/10/06/features-advantages-and-benefits-fab-statements/.

FUTURE PRESENT. 7 Ways to Introduce a New Product in a Presentation [EB/OL]. 2023-08-18. https://blog.futurepresent.agency/new-product-presentation-tips.

GLOBAL EXAM. Business English: How to Present a Company Successfully [EB/OL]. 2023-08-18. https://global-exam.com/blog/en/business-english-present-your-company-in-english/.

INDEED EDITORIAL TEAM. How to Develop a Successful Product Presentation [EB/OL]. 2023-03-11. https://www.indeed.com/career-advice/career-development/presentation-of-products.

SCHOFIELD J, OSBORN A. Collins English for Business: Speaking [M]. London: Collins, 2014.

Chapter 7

Business socializing

Socializing in business is essential because it helps business people establish relationships and earn trust from their counterparts and co-workers. It is also well-acknowledged that good relationships do not happen on their own, rather they are cultivated. In this chapter, necessary and basic communication skills for socializing at the workplace are introduced, including greetings and introductions, small talks and rules regarding business visiting.

 Learning Objectives

➢ To understand the procedures and etiquette of welcoming and receiving visitors
➢ To introduce yourself and your partners effectively at workplace
➢ To interpret the basic rules of starting small talks at workplace to improve interpersonal relation

Section 1 Workplace greetings and introductions

Greetings are vital to make the first impression, establish good relationships with others and set a positive tone for any conversation whether it is with your friend, boss or with colleagues. If you want to display a good personality, you should not ignore the importance of greetings. Delivering proper greetings to the people you come across, you can make good impact on others and climb the ladder of success sooner.

1. Non-verbal greeting protocols in the business world

Many businesses now operate within a global context so we must take account of

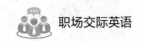

cultural diversity, both within the workplace and when travelling for business. Knowing how to meet and greet your colleagues, associates, clients, or even business superiors was once a standardized procedure which tended to be based upon where you were in the world. For instance, in the USA you'd expect a firm handshake, whereas in Japan you'd more likely receive a bowing in the business situation. In Italy, you may also likely receive a kiss on the cheeks. You may find this is really confusing, when you travel to different countries or do business with people from different areas in the world; it is unlikely for us to know what exactly their local customs and cultures are, so that it is very important for you to just focus on the business norm, which is HANDSHAKE. A handshake is appropriate when meeting a business associate in a social setting. And this is accepted for men and women in most countries and cultures.

Despite the fact that handshake is the widely accepted form of greeting in the international business world, the manner in which it is performed varies from country to country. For instance, in most Asian counties or regions, their handshake etiquette follows China's lead, that is, to grip lightly and bow slightly. Do not squeeze their hand, that's considered rude. Avoid direct eye contact and hold onto the person's hand a second or two after the handshake has finished. You should also greet the oldest people first—it's a matter of respect. In some cultures and countries, such as Brazil, France and Morocco, handshakes are usually accompanied by light kisses on the cheek, even in business situations. Western culture typically perceives a strong handshake as authoritative and confident. In parts of Northern Europe, a quick, firm handshake is the norm. In parts of Southern Europe, Central and South America, a handshake is longer and warmer, with the left hand usually touching the clasped hands or elbow. However, in some countries, such as Turkey a firm handshake is considered rude and aggressive. Men in Islamic countries never shake the hands of women outside the family.

2. Verbal greetings at workplace

Besides the non-verbal greeting, appropriate verbal greetings in situations such as Business meetings & negotiations, communicating with high-level management, saying hello to the company president or colleagues, meeting new business colleagues, clients in the office, are needed to show respect to the importance of a situation or the person to keep a professional tone. Use the example words and expressions below to appropriately greet individuals or groups and start conversations.

● **Casual/informal verbal greetings:**

With colleagues you know well, clients you have developed a relationship with or people who are acquaintances of yours (not close friends or family, but people you are friendly with), it is appropriate to be a little more relaxed with the language. You can greet them by saying:

➢ **"Hi," "Hello" and "Hey"**

"Hello" and "Hi" are very common and appropriate to use in more informal situations. Most of the time, people include the person's first name.

➢ **Hello/Hi/*Hey + the person's first name**

❖ Hi/Hello, Mary.

Notes: "Hey" should be reserved for people you know well. This is the most informal of these three greetings but it is definitely appropriate for people in your office you see every day and your close work colleagues.

➢ **How are you?/How are you doing?/How is it going?**

Most of the time, we follow "hello" or "hi" with one of these questions. These questions should have very simple answers and should be focused on the *positive or neutral*. You should not answer with a list of everything you did during the day, nor should you provide a negative answer. Appropriate answers are as follows:

❖ Fine, thanks. And you?
❖ Great! You?
❖ Good, thanks. How about you? Doing well. And how have you been?
❖ Not bad. And you? How are you?
❖ I am great, thank you for asking. How about you?
❖ I am doing alright, thank you, and you?/I'm feeling just fine, thank you and you?

Notes: Sometimes the answer is the same as the question itself and we have such situation in Business Professional greetings with "How do you do?" This is often confusing the first time you hear it or experience it. These questions can also be a greeting, not a real question. It is commonly used when passing or walking by someone you know but you have no time to talk at workplace.

● **Commonly used verbal greetings**

Besides the expressions introduced above, there are some other greeting expressions that can be used in quite formal situations:

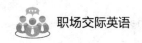

➤ **Good morning/Good afternoon/Good Evening**

This is the most common form of greeting in a formal situation and is appropriate to use anytime—with colleagues, business clients, formal relationships, new neighbors, etc. To be particularly respectful, you can also include the person's last name, for example:

➤ **Good morning/Good afternoon/Good Evening + Title + Family name**

❖ Good morning, Doctor Wang.

If you know someone well, you can also use the first name.

❖ Good morning, John.

When you are greeting a group of people—for example at a meeting—you can also say something such as:

❖ Good morning, everyone. I hope you are doing well this morning.

➤ **Hello. How do you do?**

This is used when meeting someone for the first time and is very formal. It may be used in a formal business situation or a formal dinner party event. But this is not really a "How are you?" question. It is only a simple greeting and has a similar meaning to "Nice to meet you."

➤ **Nice to meet you./Pleased to meet you.**

You are probably already familiar with these expressions from your English studies as they are common in many English books. These expressions are best used in formal or business situations when you meet someone for the first time, for example:

A: Good morning. How do you do? I'm Wang Chen with ABC company.
B: Pleased to meet you Mr. Wang.

➤ **Long-time no see.**

This expression is used when you have not seen someone for a long time. It is also a great expression to use to start a little small talk. The question "When was the last time we saw each other?" is an easy way to start a conversation about what has happened since you last saw each other.

➤ **Good to see you./It's great to see you./Nice to see you.**

You can use these expressions when you have not seen someone for a long time or when you meet someone unexpectedly. For example, meeting a client for a lunch, seeing a business contact at a meeting or seeing an acquaintance at the grocery store. These expressions can be used immediately after saying hello or hi in the greeting.

> ❖ Hello, Fang Fang, it is good to meet you.

Use as a part of your closing, after you finish a short conversation.

> ❖ Well, it is great to see you. I have to go. Have a good day. Goodbye.

> ➢ **How have you been doing?/How have you been?/How have things been going (since I last saw you)?/How have things been going (since I last saw you)?/ What have you been up to?**

These are very simple, polite and appropriate questions to use to start a conversation and can be used as a greeting after "Hi" or "Hello" in a business or formal situation. It is a respectful way to ask "How are you?" with someone you have not seen in a long time or someone you do not see every day.

 Practice and activity

1. Read the short dialogues below and answer the two questions: (1) What is their relationship in each dialogue? (2) Are the greetings formal or informal?

   a. **Mary:** Mr. Wang, How do you do? I'm Mary Ma, Personnel Officer. Welcome to our company.

     Mr. Wang: Thank you, Ms. Ma. How do you do?

   b. **Alice:** What a pleasure to see you, John! How are you doing?

     John : Not bad. How are you doing, Alice?

   c. **A:** Good afternoon, I have an appointment with David Smith.

     B: Good afternoon, could you sit down for a moment? I'll find out whether Mr. Smith is in.

     A: Thanks, I'm Mary Ma from ABC High-tech Company.

   d. **You:** Good morning, Sir!

     A: Hi, Thomas. How are you?

     You: I am very well, thank you. How are you?

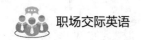

A: Fine, thank you.

2. Choose the appropriate phrases to greet each other according to the settings

a. Greet someone you have never met

b. Greet your colleague/co-worker

c. Greet your client in your company

3. Introductions

● Introducing oneself

A. How to introduce yourself at a job interview?

Introducing yourself is an important part of the interview session, which can attract the board member with an attractive introduction. A proverb says that "Smile is the best way to introduce yourself." So, as an applicant, it is better to smile while introducing yourself. Usually, they will ask you, "Tell me about yourself" or "Tell us about yourself." Your introduction usually involves:

➢ Full name

➢ Residence

➢ Educational background

➢ Career goals

➢ Experience (project, internship, co-op, etc.)

Additionally, you can also introduce your hobbies and interests and describe how well you fit in the job. The following are some examples:

Name: Greet your interviewers and tell your name to start the formal introduction. It is always a good idea to prepare for this most expected question beforehand. For instance:

❖ Good morning, I'm Andy Johnson and I'm glad to meet you.
❖ Hello, I'm Timothy Smith.
❖ It's a pleasure to meet you.
❖ Hello, my name is Wang Fang.

Residence: Mention the place you belong to, the location of your school, your college, and so on. Some people do not consider it worth mentioning, but it, surely, gives a lot about your background. Examples:

❖ I'm native to Nanjing (city/country names), but now/currently I'm studying in Xi'an.

❖ I have been born and brought up in Lanzhou. I came to Shanghai one month ago to explore professional opportunities.

❖ I stay in Shanghai with my parents/family.

❖ I'm from Xi'an/I was born and raised in Xi'an/I grew up in Xi'an.

Educational background: Give a brief account of your educational background such as your school, graduation, post-graduation and so on. Mention extra-curricular activities you have been a part of. Do not list all the courses and certifications you have done. Just include what is relevant to the specific job profile. Examples:

❖ I'm studying or I have completed my graduation or Master's degree/PhD at Tsinghua University, majoring in Electronics.

❖ I have completed the Bachelor of communication degree majoring in Journalism at Renmin University of China.

❖ I have done my schooling from Beijing. For my graduation, I chose Economics at Tsinghua University.

Experience: If you are a fresher, your educational qualifications are your asset. However, if you are experienced personnel, then you ought to mention all the particulars of your previous work experiences and all that you learned and achieved during that time. Examples:

❖ Previously, I worked at a renowned IT company/got hired by a renowned IT company through the campus placement. I have been working with the company for almost eight years now. I have learned the ins and outs of IT operations in my journey from a fresher to a manager.

❖ I have been working as a Sales Professional for 5 years now. I joined as a Sales executive and worked my way up to the position of Sales Manager within 3 years. I have a thorough understanding of Sales planning and business development. I have been mostly involved in establishing effective client relationships.

❖ I have previously worked on projects based on hardware, big data analysis and gained profound knowledge in data analysis.

If you are a fresher, then you can talk about the internships and workshops you have attended. Examples are as follow:

❖ I had internships with ABC High-tech Company where I learned how to coordinate with others and gained valuable knowledge in telecommunication.

❖ I now work as an intern at Youth Foundation.

❖ I have also worked as a part-time event coordinator and social media anchor for few local and international events.

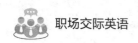

Hobbies/passion/strengths/weakness: Talk about your hobbies at length professionally and personally. Showcase your qualities and personality while mentioning your hobbies. By doing so, you can take charge of your interview. Examples:

❖ I'm a big fan of football and gymnastics.

❖ My interests lie in reading and writing.

❖ In my free time, I enjoy reading, cooking and listening to music.

❖ I love playing basketball and have represented my school in many competitions.

❖ My active participation in sports has taught me many skills.

❖ I have a fascination for languages, so I am learning the English language.

❖ I'm very good at communication.

❖ My strengths are my positive attitude, punctuality, and interpersonal skills.

❖ I think that I am an ideal candidate for this job as I found myself satisfying these requirements of the opening.

Sample self-introductions for freshers

Sample 1

Good morning. I want to thank everyone for giving me this golden opportunity to introduce myself. My name is Wang Fang and I am from Xi'an. I am an Computer Science graduate from Northwestern Polytechnical university. I now work as an intern at Youth Foundation, and I am a big fan of gymnastics and badminton. My goal is to build a successful career as an programmer, which can help the company and me personally. My strengths are my positive attitude, punctuality, and interpersonal skills. My weakness is my emotional nature. This is all about me. Thanks once again for this wonderful chance.

Sample 2

Good morning Sir/Madam:

Firstly, I would like to thank you for giving me this opportunity. I am Li Lei from Beijing. I completed my Master's degree from Tsinghua University with an aggregate of 88%. My hobbies are net surfing, playing football. I am fresher and have no work experience in any company. My strength is that I can adapt quickly to any environment.

My short-term goal is to get placed in a reputed company like yours, which will allow me to enhance my skills and knowledge. My long term goal would be to reach a higher position in your company. Finally, I think that I am an ideal candidate for this job as I found myself satisfying the requirements of this opening. That's all about me. Thank you for giving me such an excellent opportunity.

Sample self-introductions for experienced professionals

Sample 1

Good morning. I am Tim Lin, from Shaanxi. I completed my Bachelor of Engineering degree in 2009 from Northwestern Polytechnic University. I got hired by a renowned IT company through the campus placement. I have been working with the company for almost a decade now. I have learned the ins and outs of IT operations in my journey from a fresher to a manager. My qualifications and work experience make me a suitable candidate for the profile. I am looking to join your organization to explore new dimensions and for the further development of my skills. Thank you!

Sample 2

Good morning/Hello, everyone, I am Ma Li, you can call me Mar.

I am native to Shaanxi. If you talk about my educational background, I completed my Bachelor degree of Engineering in 2006. After that, I changed my line of profession and got into writing for the English language always remained my first love. I started writing for a news magazine following which I got involved in some serious kind of writing. I started preparing resumes, essays, and statements of purpose for students who aspire to go abroad for higher education. I supplemented this with blog writing where I gained exposure in or line content. Working in all these spheres gave me an overall experience in the field of content creation and editing. I want to join your organization for the further development of my skills. Thank you!

B. How to introduce yourself at workplace

When you meet people in business or at workplace for the first time, you want to create a good first impression of both yourself and your company. But you have to decide whether this is a formal or casual situation. With more formal introductions, you have to use more formal greetings and to use a title, for example, Mr., Dr., or Ms., You are more likely to use first and last names as well.

The second step is to think about the structure of your self-introduction, which is the most important and the most challenging part of the introduction, because there are some big decisions to make. Here is a question that you should ask yourself, that is, what does this person, or what do these people need to know about me?

For a new co-worker, he/she may want to know

➤ What is your position or job title in the company?

➤ What is your role or what problems do you solve in the company?

➤ If they have a problem, can they come to you to ask for help? Are you the right person?

➤ How long have you been at the company? What do you like about working there?

As you get to know your new coworker, other more personal details will become part of the conversation.

For a potential new client, he/she might be interested in:

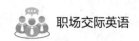

- What is your position?
- Why are they meeting with you and not someone else?
- What is your particular area of expertise or how are you going to help this potential new client solve a problem?
- How will you be able to answer any questions they have?

A meeting or an online call with peers or others in your industry, people may want to know:

- Your position or which team you're on within the company.
- Where you are located, if you're part of an international company.
- Why you are on this particular call, what expertise do you have that will be important in the conversation.

To sum up, introductions are typically short. You don't need to spend a lot of time talking about yourself. You don't need to give your entire job history. You only have to share relevant details and keep it simple.

Here are some examples:
- **Hello, I'm/my name is + your full name (formal)/your first name**

❖ Hello, I'm/My name is Ben Smith.

You may say "Hi" instead of "Hello." "Hi" may sometimes be considered to be less formal. But in general, both "Hello" and "Hi" are acceptable these days. Then you want to tell people where you work, you can talk about your company name, location and length of service. You may choose to be very general by only mentioning the company where you work.

- **I'm + your name + with/from + [company name]**

❖ I'm Wang Fang, with Bank of China/Huawei.

If you want to give more details about your job like the location, you can say
- **I'm based in + location**

❖ I'm based in London/our headquarters in Shenzhen.

Let's say someone asks you "How long have you been with this company?" (Here's one way you could phrase your answer.）

> **I've been with + [company name] + for + [length of time]**

❖ I've been with Tencent for three years.

> **I've been with + [company name] + since + [year]**

❖ I've been with Tencent since 2011.

Besides introducing your names and companies, you could also offer some details about your job responsibilities. For instance:

> **I'm responsible for + [verb]ing + [area of responsibility]**

❖ I'm responsible for ensuring that our new staff are well trained.

> **I head the + [department/project]**

❖ I head the sales department/engineering project.

> **I manage the + [department/project]**

❖ I manage the finance department/the sales project team.

> **I look after + [department/project]**

❖ I look after the HR department/all the pubs in this state.

> **I'm in charge of + [department/project]**

❖ I'm in charge of the marketing department/the hotel construction project.

> **I report (directly) to the + [superior]**

❖ I report (directly) to the CFO.

- **Introducing others**

When you are introducing two or more people to each other, a great introduction can lead to a meaningful discussion and a lasting connection being built. When you introduce people who do not know each other, you should:

> State the name of the person you are introducing.

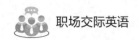
➢ Inform them of your intent.

➢ Sate the name of the person who is being introduced.

➢ Offer additional information, as appropriate.

Here are some examples:

● **Names and intent**

➢ **A, I'd like you to meet B (formal)/A, this is B (less formal).**

❖ Xiao Wang, I'd like you to meet Mr. Henry Zhang./Xiao Wang, this is Henry.

➢ **A, let me introduce you to B.**

❖ Xiao Zhang, let me introduce you to President Ma.

Some other expressions can be used to inform others while you are making an introduction:

❖ Can/May I introduce a good friend of mine?

❖ This is...Have you met...

❖ I want you to meet...

❖ I would like you to meet...

❖ It's a pleasure to introduce…

❖ I would like to introduce...

❖ I would like to present...

❖ May I present...

❖ This is...

● **State the name of the person who is being introduced**

After informing the parties of your intent to make an introduction, state the name of the person you are introducing. In most situations, this is usually the younger person, one who has a lower-ranking title or who you know the least about. If you are introducing more than two people to each other, state the name of each person in ranking order beginning with the highest rank and working your way down.

● **Offer additional information, as appropriate**

You can offer both parties information about each other that can help them establish a connection or begin a conversation, for instance, offer the job positions and the purposes of the introduction.

Here are some examples:

➢ **Mention their jobs:**

> ❖ She's in charge of our marketing division.
> ❖ He is from Human Resources.
> ❖ She's our sales representative.
> ❖ He manages.../He heads...

➢ **The purpose of the introduction:**

> ❖ She will be joining us today. (She will stay at our meeting.)
> ❖ She will be sitting in...
> ❖ He is going to stay for some time.

Examples of introductions

Here are a few examples of good introductions you can use in a variety of situations:

➢ **Introducing professionals or colleagues of different ranks**

When you are introducing business professionals or colleagues of different ranks to each other, it is usually best to introduce the person who has the least amount of experience or who has the lower-ranking title within the organization or industry to the person who has the most amount of experience or who has the higher-ranking title. For instance:

> ❖ Mr. Johnson, I would like you to meet Ms. Jenny Wang. Ms. Wang is joining our organization as an administrative assistant. Jenny, Mr. Johnson has been with our organization since its founding ten years ago. He started in an entry level position and is now our sales director.

➢ **Introducing a business professional to a customer or client**

When you are introducing a business colleague to a customer or client, always begin by addressing the customer or client first. This is the professional standard even when you are introducing them to high-ranking members within your organization. For instance:

> ❖ Miss Lee, I am pleased to introduce our head of account management, Mrs. Wu to you. Mrs. Wu, Miss Lee has just signed a one-year contract with our organization for social media management and content creation for the local restaurant she owns.

➢ **Introducing people in casual and social settings**

When you are introducing friends, colleagues or family members to each other in a casual or social setting, it is better to introduce the person you have known for the least

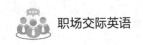

amount of time or that you know the least about to the person you have known the longest or with whom you have a stronger personal connection. For instance:

> ❖ Mom, I would like you to meet my friend, Heather. We met in our after-school Junior Chemists Club and have become good friends since. Heather, this is my mom, she has been a teacher of English for 30 years and is the person who inspired my passion for English.

➢ Introducing one person to a group of people

When you are introducing one person to a group of people, the order of introduction may not begin with the highest-ranking person. Instead, it is common to begin these introductions by first addressing the group and then introducing them to the individual person. For instance:

> ❖ Ladies and gentlemen, it is my pleasure to introduce you to the Founder and CEO of Tasty Sweets, Mr. Richard Smith.

In each of the above examples, the person who is being introduced is the higher-ranking individual. But beginning the introductions by addressing the group first will draw the attention of the entire group before introducing individuals.

4. Etiquette: Protocol of introducing people

The purpose of introducing people is to give them an opportunity to know each other. Beyond just stating names of the two parties, the person making the introduction is often obligated to establish an acquaintance and help the two parties initiate a conversation. The foremost principle of etiquette for making introductions lies in understanding reverence and respect. The basic protocol of introductions calls for introducing the "lesser-ranking" (socially, professionally, by age or seniority) to the "higher-ranking" person. Here are some guidelines.

Basic protocol: introduce the "lower-ranking" to the "higher-ranking"		
Higher-ranking	**Lower-ranking**	**Example**
An older person	A younger person	Grandpa, this is my neighbour, Jane.
A senior professional	A junior professional	Mr. President, this is my secretary.
A customer	A team of employees	Mr. Customer, this is my sales team.
A guest	A host	Hi, Ms. Wang, this is my daughter, Sarah.
A guest from out-of-town	A local host	Mr. Lee, this is my neighbour Jason.
Peer from another company	Peer from your company	Mr. Anderson, this is Ms. Edwards.

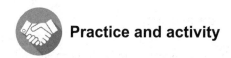

Practice and activity

1. Use a sentence to describe the responsibilities of the following jobs, an example is given below:

I'm a nurse. *I help to look after people when they are sick.*

I'm a scientist._____

I work in the HR department._____

I'm a barber._____

I'm a vet._____

I'm a fashion designer._____

2. Suppose that you are going to graduate and looking for a job. You are at a job interview and the interviewers ask you to give a self-introduction. You have to briefly introduce.

➢ Who you are

➢ Where you are from

➢ What you study

➢ Why you think that you are qualified for the job

Section 2　Making small talk at the workplace with colleagues and coworkers

Small talk is the common term for a conversation about light and unimportant matters. It is vital for situations where silence would be awkward and uncomfortable, but where in-depth and personal conversations would be inappropriate. Small talk is a short conversation. Basically, small talk in general is a communication skill, which is a short friendly conversation about a common topic. Small talk can take place among friends, co-workers, or strangers. But it is not small. Making small talk is an essential communication skill. These brief, casual conversations are a great way to get to know new people, but they can be even more important in the workplace. If you're working in a traditional office where you get to see your coworkers every day, there are so many opportunities for you to interact, for instance, walking through the hallway, passing by their offices, stopping by their desks, in the kitchen, or the cafeteria.

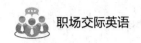

Importance of making small talks in business setting

Small talk is a cornerstone of building rapport, which is important in both business and personal scenarios. Good small talk skills can help:

➢ **To create a bond:** By opening up your interests, you can create a more personal bond with someone and therefore a better relationship.

➢ **To create a network:** Having strong small talk skills can help you meet new people, form positive business relationships and open new career opportunities. For instance, making small talk in the workplace can even help you get access to more job opportunities because your coworkers will have a chance to get to know you.

➢ **To create a positive atmosphere:** You can use small talk to make yourself and others feel at ease.

1. Making small talk

Many businesses and companies have clear guidelines about subject matter that is not deemed appropriate for discussion in the workplace. There are some topics which are very personally sensitive or the topics may cause someone to become upset, thus should be avoided in small talk.

➢ **Religion and politics:** These topics can be very personal and quickly lead to arguments if people disagree, so it's best to avoid them in a business setting.

➢ **Life and death:** Any recent health scares or chronic problems are not appropriate small talk topics. When you are in the presence of strangers, stay clear of topics that could potentially be upsetting.

➢ **Appearance and/or age:** Never make personal comments about someone's appearance. Even if you think you are being complimentary, it could make them feel uncomfortable since successful small talk is all about creating a relaxed atmosphere. Don't ask anyone's age either—this can be a very sensitive topic.

➢ **Family/relationship status:** It's okay to ask about someone's family only if you already know them. If something negative happens on your colleagues in their family, this topic can create bad feelings between you and the other person.

➢ **Personal comments:** Don't badmouth others, especially in a business context! It can make you look untrustworthy, and could damage relationships further down the line.

➢ **Money/anything financial:** It is inappropriate to tell others how much money you make or ask them how much money they make or talk about bonuses or anything financial. These topics should be avoided. You should also avoid gossiping about the financial situations of co-workers or managers.

➢ **Jokes:** Some jokes may be okay if they're clean and inoffensive. However, don't tell potentially offensive jokes that involve racism, sexism, violence, and other inappropriate workplace topics.

As mentioned above, being able to make small talk will help you show interest in your coworkers and build stronger work relationships. You have to avoid the topics which are inappropriate as aforementioned. Topics which are safe and appropriate are as follows:

➢ **Weather/climate:** It's a cliché but people are generally happy to talk about the weather/climate, even if it can seem rather mundane. Plus it's completely inoffensive and allows everyone to have something to say. Leading with a question is ideal as it naturally starts a conversation. For instance, you can ask about the other person's plans given the weather. Here are some examples:

❖ If it is rainy, are you going to stay at home and watch movies?
❖ If it is sunny, are you going to have a BBQ, do something outdoorsy, or go on a hike?

You can also discuss their favorite type of climate/weather and why they like it. This frequently turns into a discussion about their personality, which can be fun and interesting. In addition, you can also get them talking about the climate/weather in their hometown. For instance:

❖ Is the weather different from where you live now?
❖ Which type of climate do you enjoy more?
❖ If you could choose to live anywhere based solely on the weather conditions, where would it be?

Here are some more expressions:

❖ What was the weather like in Xi'an—when you left?
❖ Terrible. I'm hoping to bring back some of this sunshine with me.
❖ It's a beautiful day, isn't it?
❖ Glorious! Is it always this nice?
❖ Is it true it always rains in the UK?
❖ Well, it definitely rains a lot but we do have the odd nice day.

➢ **Travel/tourism:** People love to talk about their vacation plans, where they have been

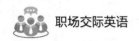

and where they are planning to go. Show interest and the conversation should flow. It is possible that not everyone you speak with will be a world traveler, but asking if they've traveled anywhere interesting lately can open up a world of possibilities. You have to make sure that you have some follow-up questions around what they plan to do on their trip. Here are a few examples of how to begin a small talk on traveling with some open-ended questions:

- ❖ Do you know any places locally that might be considered "hidden gems"?
- ❖ What foods are you most excited to try?
- ❖ What souvenirs are you planning to bring home.
- ❖ If you could vacation anywhere, where would you go and why?
- ❖ Where was your last vacation to?
- ❖ Describe your dream vacation.
- ❖ Do you have recommendations for airlines?

> **Food/restaurants/cooking:** Food is a fail-safe topic of conversation, since almost everyone loves to eat. Try these food questions to get the conversation started:

- ❖ What's your favorite type of food?
- ❖ What wine would you pair with this food and why?
- ❖ If you could only eat one food forever, what food would you pick and why?
- ❖ What's a food that a lot of people think is unappetizing but you really like?
- ❖ What's a weird food you've eaten?
- ❖ What's your favorite thing to cook at home?
- ❖ What's your favorite restaurant and why? What's a food you will not eat?
- ❖ Tell me about your go-to comfort food.

> **Sports:** Some people could talk about sports all day. Others would rather talk about anything but sports. There are a few rules of thumb for discussing sports. First, if you're in a group of two-plus people, make sure everyone is a sports fan. You don't want to exclude someone from participating. Second, while an enthusiastic conversation is fun, a heated one won't help your networking goals whatsoever. If you or the other person starts getting riled up, change the topic. Here are some examples that you can follow:

- ❖ Did you watch the Champions League final?
- ❖ Of course it was a fantastic game and that last goal was unbelievable!
- ❖ Do you do much sport yourself?

> ❖ I sometimes play paddle at the weekend. How about you? Your country's famous for football isn't it?
> ❖ Yes, but we're also interested in basketball and hockey. Lots of people are really into cycling at the moment too.

➤ **Entertainment:** Talk about what you've enjoyed lately and what's on your list. That might include the show either of you are binge-watching, the last movie each of you saw, the books you're reading, the podcasts you're streaming, any plays you've attended, and so on. Here are some examples:

> ❖ Do you have recommendations for books?
> ❖ What's your favorite band/song? Why?
> ❖ What are your favorite movies?
> ❖ What's a movie that came out this year that I need to see? Why?
> ❖ What's a book/movie/TV show you didn't like despite everyone else seeming to enjoy it?
> ❖ What are you currently streaming?
> ❖ What's a movie that recently made you laugh?
> ❖ Name a movie that recently made you cry.
> ❖ If you could only choose one streaming series to watch forever, which would it be?
> ❖ What are your must-have phone apps?

➤ **Work:** Talking about your day jobs can be tricky. You don't want the conversation to devolve into a boring comparison of what you do. On the other hand, work is a good small talk topic because the vast majority of people have something to say. Instead of asking generic questions like, "Where do you work?" "How long have you worked there?" and "Do you like it?" use interesting ones and you can start by asking if they've been in their current position for long or how they got into their line of work. Always show an interest in the other person, ask questions rather than talking about yourself, and don't start with a business request or a hard sell. For instance:

> ❖ What projects are keeping you busy these days?
> ❖ What are you currently working on?
> ❖ What's some great career advice you've received?
> ❖ My [niece/son/grandchild] wants: to become a [profession]. Do you have any advice I should pass on?
> ❖ What's your favorite aspect of your job? Why did you decide to work in (X field)?
> ❖ Which skill do you use the most in your work? Is that what you expected?
> ❖ What's the stereotype of a (job title)? Does it hold up?
> ❖ Is there anything you didn't anticipate about this role? Do you like or dislike that?

Tips: Be Careful When Discussing Work! You should always try to be positive when discussing work. You never know if a more senior colleague is listening to what you are saying.

Procedures: English small talk at workplace

➢ **Step one: Start the talk with greetings.** Most conversations begin with a greeting. In English you'll find formal and informal greetings that can be used in various situations.

❖ Hello!
❖ Good morning/Good afternoon/Good evening.
❖ My name is.../I'm...and I work for...
❖ Nice to meet you, (name).
❖ Good to see you!

➢ **Step two: Choose a topic (hobbies, entertainment).** After the greeting you can choose topics that are safe and appropriate to start a small talk. For example:

❖ What do you like to do during your spare time?
❖ Do you do any sports?
❖ Are you reading any good books right now? I'd like some recommendations.

➢ **Step three: Listen and respond.** You need to listen to the other people in the group and respond to what they are saying. You can often use short phrases to respond to someone else. These can show that you agree or understand their comments, that you are paying attention or used to compliment the other person. For example:

❖ Uh-huh.	❖ That is interesting!
❖ Oh, really?	❖ Oh, I see.
❖ That sounds great!	❖ Oh, wow!

➢ **Step four: Ask others in the group.** You don't have to change the topic and ask more questions every time you speak. If you have a group of people, you can simply ask the same question to other people as well as sharing opinions.

❖ What do you think?
❖ And how about you?
❖ And you?
❖ What's your opinion?

> ➤ **Step five: Close the talk.** Hopefully, you will get to know some interesting people at business events, but English small talk must, sooner or later, come to an end. Here are some useful expressions to close a conversation:

❖ It was great/nice to meet you.

❖ It was a pleasure meeting you.

❖ I look forward to seeing you again.

❖ Let's keep in touch.

2. Tips to help small talk flow more smoothly

It doesn't matter how poor you are at small talk. With practice and the right strategies, you can improve. Here are some strategies that can help you get better at small talk:

- **Ask open-ended questions**

These invite the respondent to reveal information and keep the conversation flowing. An example could be, "What do you think about the proposed merger?"

- **Take note of your body language**

Make necessary eye contact throughout the conversation, smile and look interested.

- **Prepare before the event**

If you know you have an important meeting coming up and want to make a good impression, a bit of preparation helps.

- **Greet people appropriately**

In business, a firm handshake is a safe bet unless you are meeting international clients. If in the office with your colleagues, it is not very formal to start the conversations like this. You can start the conversation with a positive attitude through your tone of voice to help them feel more ready to engage with you.

- **Remember names**

Sometimes name tags are used to help people network, with that person's role and company stated. If they're not used, try to say someone's name a couple of times in the conversation shortly after you have been introduced, to help remember it.

- **Dealing with silences**

Not all silences are bad; sometimes lulls in conversation just indicate that a person is considering what to say next or is thinking about what you have told them. If you feel the silences are prolonged, then try to change the topic of conversation or ask some questions.

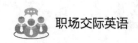

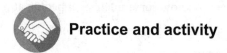 **Practice and activity**

Role-play: Suppose you are in the following situations, how can you start small talk? Use what has been introduced above in this chapter and practice with your partners.

A. You are walking down the corridor of your company and bump into an old friend, who is also your acquaintance. What will you say to him?

B. You are sitting in the company's cafeteria, enjoying a cup of coffee, when a colleague just comes and sits next to you. What will you say to him?

Section 3　Business visits

1. Welcoming visitors

Meeting in person can be very important to business relationships. It's a chance to make connections and build rapport. In particular, when you have visitors from different cultures, it is very important to make them feel at home. Usually after the greeting and self-introduction, you can have a small talk with them.

Here are some great ways to start a conversation with your visitor:

➢ **Ask them if they know the area**

❖ Have you been to China before?
❖ Is this your first time in Xi'an?

➢ **Give some advice about where to eat**

❖ I can suggest an excellent local restaurant that serves pita bread in mutton soup which is a local dish!
❖ I know a great local restaurant, they have the best roasted lamb.

If you want to invite your business guest to dinner (or lunch) you can say:

❖ Would you like to join me for dinner?

2. Company guided visits

After the small talk, the visitors might want to visit your office/company and take a tour, and they might be a prospective client who wants to see where the products are made, or perhaps someone from head office is on an inspection tour, or it could be an official inspection to make sure you are following government or internal standards. Taking visitors to your company on a tour requires a certain amount of planning. You should prepare the route and the duration of the visit.

- **Expressions of introduction for a company visit in English**
  - ➤ **Greeting and general introduction**

❖ Good morning, ladies and gentlemen. Could I have your attention, please? Welcome to (X company). My name is...and I'm going to give you a tour of the offices/company/factory. The tour will last about thirty minutes. (Formal visit for larger groups.)

❖ Good morning, nice to meet you. I'm... Come with me and I'll show you around. The tour will just take thirty minutes. (A less formal visit for individuals and very small groups. You should also ask names if you have not been introduced.)

❖ If you would like to follow me, we will begin our tour of the premises.

❖ Please, follow me.

❖ Let me show you around the office.

  - ➤ **Talking about the directions**

❖ In front of you is...

❖ On your right, you will see...

❖ Up ahead and to your left, you will see...

❖ As we turn the corner here, you will see...

❖ In the distance...

❖ If you look behind me, now...

❖ If you look up you will notice...

❖ Off to the north...

❖ Look to the east…

❖ To the west...

❖ We are now coming up to...

❖ As you will see...

  - ➤ **Talking about the history of the company**

❖ The company was founded in (year) by (founder's name).

❖ The company was the brainchild of (name).

❖ The company was started by (name) at the end of the nineteenth century.

❖ In the early days...

❖ In those days, the company was based in (place name). It was transferred to its present location 6 years later.

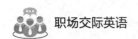

❖ The company was the first to announce the development of...

❖ It delivered the first (product name) in March of 1973.

❖ Since its inception, this company has led the field in the area of (company activity).

❖ In 1990, the takeover of (company name) located at (place name) took place.

❖ In 2000, the company was relocated from (place name) to (new place name) and began production of new products.

❖ Today, (company name) occupies a leading position for (service or product name) solutions in different sectors of the market.

➤ **Describing buildings, offices etc:**

❖ Our offices are on the 28th and the 29th floors of this building called (building name).

❖ It is very well situated for staff and visitors with the train station at just a five-minute walk away and a taxi-rank almost opposite the front entrance.

❖ There is ample parking space for employees and visitors below the building and close to the park area next to it.

❖ There are ample garden areas around the premises where staff can relax and have a coffee during breaks.

❖ There are over 25 offices here at (company name). There are also 500 square meters of open plan office.

❖ On the floor below this one, there is a small gymnasium exclusively for company staff and visitors with all-day opening hours.

❖ Apart from the offices, there are also 2 reception areas, 4 conference rooms fully equipped with the latest video-conferencing machines, communal rest areas with kitchenettes, and a cafeteria area with seating for 50 people.

❖ Lunches are provided from 13:30 to 15:30 at very economical prices if you're interested after the tour!

❖ There are toilets to our right if you would like to take advantage of time before I begin the tour of the offices.

● **Expressions for ending the company visit**

➤ **More formal expressions for larger groups**

❖ Well, that concludes our tour. I hope you have enjoyed it and have found it interesting and informative. If you have any further questions, I should be very happy to answer them now.

❖ On behalf of (company name) and myself, I should like to thank you all for visiting us today. I wish you all a very pleasant journey home.

➤ **Less formal expressions for small groups**

❖ So, that's the end of our tour. I hope you've enjoyed it. Can I help you with any last questions?

❖ Thanks for visiting us today. I hope you have a good trip home.

➢ **Welcome guests/visitors to your company/office**

Knowing how to welcome business visitors is an important speaking skill. This is often the first impression that a visitor will have of a company so you need to make a good impression. When visitors come, you should treat them in a friendly and relaxed manner, and make sure they are comfortable if they have to wait around. Take an interest in who they are and what they've been doing. Whenever any visitor arrives, it is the responsibility of the host to approach and meet the guest with a smile, have frequent eye contact and with proper body posture. The host or employee should use very brief but welcoming phrases to greet the guest like:

> ❖ Good morning/Good afternoon/Good evening, Sir/Madam. Welcome to (company name). How may I help you?

After greeting, you as the host can offer the guest/visitor a seat and refreshments in the reception area. Some expressions are as follows:

> ❖ Would you like to take a seat?
> ❖ Would you like some tea/coffee while you wait?
> ❖ Milk and sugar?
> ❖ Can I get you anything for drink?
> ❖ Can I get you anything else?

 Practice and activity

A group of your clients from another city will visit your company for the very first time, please arrange a company tour for them.

 References

AFZAL A. How to Meet and Greet for Business Around the World [EB/OL]. 2020-01-24. https://creativeword.uk.com/blog/language/meet-greet-business-around-world/.

AGARWAL M. How to Greet your Boss/People in Office? [EB/OL]. 2013-07-15. https://english.eagetutor.com/spoken-english/628-how-to-greet-your-boss-people-in-office.html.

BELLUDI N. Etiquette: Protocol of Introducing People [EB/OL]. 2007-11-03. https://www.rightattitudes.com/2007/11/03/etiquette-protocol-introducing-people/.

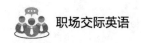

BIRT J. How to Do Introductions (With Examples and Tips) [EB/OL]. 2023-03-11. https://www.indeed.com/career-advice/interviewing/how-to-do-introductions

ENGLISH RADER. 5 Tips to Make Business English Small Talk Conversations Easier [EB/OL]. 2023-08-18. https://www.englishradar.com/work/5-tips-to-make-business-english-small-talk-conversations-easier/.

HAMEL M. Making Small Talk in Business Settings [EB/OL]. 2023-08-18. https://study.com/academy/lesson/making-small-talk-in-business-settings.html#:~:text=Basically%2C%20small%20talk%20is%20a,work%20without%20getting%20too%20personal.

HARNESS J. Proper Business Etiquette for Greeting People [EB/OL]. 2019-05-08. https://bizfluent.com/way-5860572-proper-business-etiquette-greeting-people.html.

INDEED EDITORIAL TEAM. How to Introduce Yourself Professionally (With Examples) [EB/OL]. 2023-08-01. https://www.indeed.com/career-advice/career-development/introduce-yourself-professionally/.

KITLUM. 32 Important English Phrases for Nailing Business Introductions [EB/OL]. 2023-07-27. https://www.fluentu.com/blog/business-english/business-english-introductions/#toc_6.

KHAN N. How to Introduce Someone in English: Formal & Informal [EB/OL]. 2023-03-14. https://esladvice.com/introducing-someone/.

MUNOZ P. How to Introduce People [EB/OL]. 2023-03-14. https://www.wikihow.com/Introduce-People.

SITES AT PENN STATE. Handshake Etiquette Around the World [EB/OL]. 2016-04-18. https://sites.psu.edu/tetirclblog/2016/04/18/handshake-etiquette-around-the-world/.

SOUTH AFRICA. Handshakes in Different Cultures [EB/OL]. 2018-02-15. https://www.southafrica.net/gl/en/trade/welcome/tip/handshakes-in-different-cultures.

THOMPSON S. Cultural Differences in Body Language to be Aware of [EB/OL]. 2022-09-08. https://virtualspeech.com/blog/cultural-differences-in-body-language.

WIKIJOB TEAM. The Best Ways to Make Business Small Talk (2023 Guide) [EB/OL]. 2023-06-11. https://www.wikijob.co.uk/features/useful-resources/best-ways-make-business-small-talk#tips-to-help-small-talk-flow-more-smoothly.

WILL. How to Start a Conversation in English: A Guide to Small Talk [EB/OL]. 2023-08-18. https://englishlive.ef.com/blog/language-lab/start-conversation-english-guide-small-talk/.

ZIGSAW BLOG. Self Introduction in English for Interview for Freshers [EB/OL]. 2020-10-12. https://www.zigsaw.in/jobs/self-introduction-in-english-for-interview-for-freshers/.

Chapter 8

Telephone communication

Telephone communication is one of the most important forms of communication within the company. Although today its use is being replaced by other forms of communication (such as e-mail), phone use is one of the most common means to materialize both internal and external communications. The telephone offers a faster interaction than e-mail, is more personal, and easy and quick to use. Hence, having effective telephone skills leaves a good impression on your customers, clients, and colleagues. Since people at workplace are all busy, you want to be very clear, polite and organized.

 Learning Objectives

➢ Learn to make and receive phone calls that commonly occur in the professional environment using appropriate language
➢ Understand basic etiquette in telephone communication
➢ Properly apply verbal and non-verbal communication techniques to establish friendly interpersonal relations

Section 1　Business telephone procedures

Business telephone conversations usually follow certain procedures, namely introduction, development and closure. Each procedure contains the following steps:

- **Introduction**
➢ Someone answers the phone and asks if they can help.
➢ The caller makes a request: either to be connected to someone or for information.

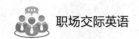

- **Development**

  ➤ The caller is connected, given information or told that they are not in the office at the moment.

  ➤ If the person who is requested is not in the office, the caller is asked to leave a message.

  ➤ The caller leaves a message or asks other questions.

- **Closure**

  ➤ End the call politely.

1. Receiving/answering phone calls

Receiving a call is probably the easiest, but in order not to make the caller feel like that he/she is bothering you, you have to make some preparations and follow the basic patterns and rules.

  ➤ Greet the caller with warm and professional greetings.

  ➤ Identify yourself/your department/company.

  ➤ Offer helps: be enthusiastic.

Here are some useful expressions:

❖ Hello, ABC Company this is Peter speaking. How may I be of help to you today?

❖ Good morning Customer Service, Wilson and Wilson. Can I help you?

❖ Tencent, this is Joe Chan speaking.

❖ Good morning/afternoon company X.

❖ Hello, this is...of company X.

❖ This is...here/This is...speaking.

❖ How can I help you?/What can I do for you?

❖ Company X, how may I help you?

There are some other expressions used in different situations, for instance:

Getting the name of the caller if he/she doesn't give it to you, you can say:

❖ May I have your name please?

❖ Who am I speaking with?

❖ Hello. May I ask who's calling?

❖ Who's speaking, please?

❖ Could you please tell me who this is?/Who is calling?

The person wanted is not there, the expressions are:

❖ I'm afraid...is not available right now/not in today.

❖ I'm afraid...is unavailable at the moment.

❖ X (name) is away for a few days./X (name) has just gone out./X (name) is out for lunch.

❖ I'm afraid...is on sickleave/on a paternity leave.

❖ X (name) is out of town/out of the office.

Responding to a caller's request, you can say:

❖ Sure, let me check on that.

❖ Let me see if she's available.

❖ Sure, one moment please.

Sometimes you need to ask someone to wait on the line and if the calls need to be on hold, please follow the procedures:

➢ Seek permission.

➢ Explain the reason.

➢ Wait for the customer's response.

➢ Get back to the customer in the committed time frame.

Here are some useful expressions:

❖ Mr. Sun, the extension is busy, may I please place your call on hold?

❖ Thank you for holding, Mr. Sun, the extension is still busy, would you like to continue holding or shall I ask Mr. Wang to call you back as soon as his extension is free?

❖ I'm sorry, but the number's engaged/the line is busy. Would you like to hold?

❖ Hold on please./Just hold the line for a second. Can I put you on hold for a minute?

❖ Do you mind holding while I check on that/handle that for you/check to see if he's available?

2. Rules for receiving/answering phone calls

Even in these days of texting and email, the phone is still most business's primary means of contacting with customers, and the way your company's phone is answered/made will form your customer's first impression of your business. Here is how to receive/answer the phone properly:

- **Answering the phone within three rings**

Responding within three rings in order to give yourself enough time to get in the zone and prepare for the call. Picking up the phone right away might leave you flustered.

- **Consider your tone**

Keep your voice at a medium level, and speak slowly enough so that the caller can easily understand what you're saying. Be friendly and smile.

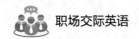

- **Announce yourself**

When answering the phone, welcome callers by greeting them and introducing yourself and the organization; this lets people know that they've dialed the right number—rather than answering with a simple "Hello".

- **Actively listen and take notes**

Listen more than you speak, especially when you're answering an incoming customer service call, and it is helpful to take notes during support calls.

- **Use proper language**

Always be mindful and respectful when on the phone. It's best to use formal language. It's okay to throw in humor if appropriate, but never crack a joke that could upset a customer.

- **Summarize key points before hanging up**

Before you sign off, make a point of summing up the call. For one, this builds some goodwill between you and the caller, as this shows you were listening to what they had to say. The summary is also a great way to make sure nothing important was missed and gives them a chance to clarify the message if needed.

- **End on a professional note**

After you summarize the bullet points of the call, make sure you end things on a professional note. Thank the caller for their time or business. You can also keep the lines of communication open. Say something like "If you need anything else, feel free to reach out."

Section 2   Making phone calls

Compared with answering phone calls, making phone calls is a little nerve-wracking. But to make the call as effective as possible, you need to identify its purpose before you pick up the phone, and keep this in mind while you talk. There are some preparations that need to be done.

1. Preparing for a call

- **Identify the specific purpose of your call**

Knowing exactly why you want to speak with someone will stop you from feeling nervous about bothering them or wasting their time. Before you make the call, reflect for a minute on its purpose. For instance, you might think:

➢ Do you need to get information?

➢ Do you want to sell something, or convince the person of an idea?

➢ Do you need to ask for the person's help or support?

- **Prepare bullet points for the things you need to mention**

Having an agenda for what you want to talk about will help keep your call on track. The "cheat sheet" can also help you feel more confident. For instance, if you are calling to ask someone for a meeting, you might jot down:

> ➢ The purpose of the meeting.
> ➢ When and where the meeting will be held.
> ➢ What the person might need to do before the meeting.

- **Research the person you need to call**

This is especially important if you don't know the caller personally. Find out what you can know about him/her from colleagues, internet searches, social media profiles, etc. If you know a bit about the person's background, you can use this knowledge for chit-chatting at the start of the call. Researching the caller also helps you avoid faux pas. For example, if you find out that the person has ties to one of your competitors, you'd make sure not to criticize that competitor.

When the call is connected, you have to keep your conversations purposefully.

2. Keeping the conversations purposefully

- **Start with some banter, but don't overdo it**

Call the number, and expect it to ring a few times before the person picks up. Greet and introduce yourself, where you're calling from and who you want to talk to. For example:

> ❖ Hello, this is Sally from Thomas Electronics, I'd like to speak to Mr. Wilson if he's available, please.
> ❖ Good morning, it is Xin Zhang from ABC company, may I speak to Mr. Wang please?

Here are some more useful phrases for greeting and asking for someone on the phone:

> ❖ Hello, this is...
> ❖ Good morning, my name is...from...
> ❖ Good morning, it is...here.
> ❖ Is Mr. Wilson available, please?
> ❖ Could I speak to...if he's available?
> ❖ Could you put me through to...?
> ❖ I'd like to speak to...if possible, please.
> ❖ Can/May I speak to...please?
> ❖ I am calling to find out about...
> ❖ Could I please speak with whoever deals with the accounts?

職场交际英语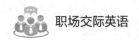

- **Get down to business of your call**

When you are talking to the person on the phone, it is polite to start with a bit of chit-chat, especially if you know the person, but don't ramble on. Keep it to just a minute or so. Then you have to shift to the real purpose of your call. But you cannot make the transition too abrupt or obvious. Try to make a smooth shift to the purpose of your call, like:

> ❖ Well, it's great to catch you up Mary. I'm calling to...
> ❖ I'm glad to hear that you're doing well. I'm calling to...

- **Make sure to ask questions**

If you just bombard the person with information, it will feel like the call is overwhelming and one-sided. Instead, stop and ask questions now and then to make the person feel included and to establish a connection. For instance:

> ❖ We're thinking of scheduling a group meeting on the 28th. How does that sound to you, Mary?
> ❖ We're hoping to get all of the branch department heads together to discuss strategy for the next quarter. Do you have any ideas for that, Mary?

- **Take notes during the call**

Jotting things down as you talk to the person has several benefits. It can help you listen attentively to anything the caller says.

- **Clarify any follow-up actions that are necessary**

If you need to find out any information and get back to the person, make a note of this. Likewise, if you need the person to do anything and get back to you later, make sure they understand this. For example, you might say:

> ❖ So Kate, I'll check with our suppliers about a time frame for delivery, and get back to you on that, OK?
> ❖ OK, Justin, if you can check your schedule and get back to me with some potential meeting times by the end of the week, that would be great, OK?

3. Rules for making a call

The rules that allow us to make successful telephone calls and to create a good image of our company and ourselves are the following:

> ➤ Make the courtesy call from a moderately quiet area using a company phone. Insure good call quality by verifying that you have a good signal if calling from a company

cell phone.

➤ Dial the number and wait for the party to answer. Wait for the client to say, "Hello" then speak. Identify yourself and the company you represent. Ask what time is best to reach him or her if the person you want to talk to is not available.

➤ Verify that you are speaking to the correct party. Say, "May I speak to Mr. Smith?" If the answering party hesitates, say, "This is a courtesy call and it will only take a minute." Wait for the party to come on the line or ask for a good call back time. If you are calling somebody back, you must state when you were called.

➤ Provide the service by giving or requesting the required information. Be polite and helpful during the call. Keep the call brief and succinct. The courtesy call should always be a method of communication that helps the customer in some way.

➤ Thank the customer for his time and remind him of how he can contact you if he has further questions.

4. Telephone messages

If the person called is not available, the caller can choose to leave a message and the person who answers the phone can ask whether the caller needs to leave a message:

- **As a recipient, you may say:**

❖ Would you like to leave a message?
❖ Could I take a message for you?
❖ Do you have a message for Mr. Evans (the caller)?

- **As a caller, you may say:**

❖ Would you mind if I leave a message?
❖ Could I possibly leave a message?
❖ I'd like to leave a message, if I can.
❖ May I leave a message for him?
❖ Can I leave a message?

Messages should include the following information:

➤ The date and time of the call.
➤ The full name of the caller (ask for correct spelling).
➤ The name of the business.
➤ A phone number to return the call.
➤ The purpose of the call.

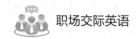

Sample conversation about taking a message

❖ **Receptionist:** A&B Importers. Good Morning. How can I help you?

❖ **Caller:** Could I speak to Mr. Jones, please? I'm calling about a meeting we have scheduled tomorrow.

❖ **Receptionist:** I am sorry, Mr. Jones is out of the office until around 3:00 pm. I can take a message and pass those details on to him as soon as he gets back if you'd like!

❖ **Caller:** That sounds great. My name is David Eddings. Mr. Jones and I are to have a meeting at 10 am tomorrow, but I will be about 20 minutes late due to an unexpected change. He can reach me at 553-546-2324.

❖ **Receptionist:** OK, 20 minutes late for the meeting. Mr. Eddings. Could you spell your name to me please?

❖ **Caller:** Certainly, David Eddings, E-D-D-I-N-G-S.

❖ **Receptionist:** Thank you, Mr. Eddings. May I check the number with you again? That is 553-546-2324.

❖ **Caller:** Yes, that's right.

❖ **Receptionist:** OK, Mr. Eddings, I will give Mr. Jones the message.

❖ **Caller:** Thanks for your help. Goodbye.

❖ **Receptionist:** Goodbye.

When you leave a message, please bear the following points in mind:

➢ Don't speak too fast.
➢ Pronounce and spell your name clearly.
➢ Slow down when saying your telephone number and pause some where.
➢ Provide your number.
➢ Give your company name, title and reason for calling.
➢ Let them know when to call you back.

During the conversation, if the caller is speaking too quickly, you can ask them to speak more slowly or repeat what they have said:

❖ Sorry, Sir. Could you say that again, please?
❖ I'm afraid I didn't catch that, Ma'am. Could you repeat it?
❖ I'm sorry. Could you say that again more slowly?
❖ Would you mind speaking more slowly, please?

Perhaps the caller has a name or company name you are not familiar with. Just ask:

❖ Could you spell your name, please?
❖ How do you spell your name, please?
❖ Would you mind spelling that, please?
❖ Would you repeat your name, please?

When getting ready to end a call, there are a few ways to reassure the caller that the message will be passed on (unless the caller has been transferred already to voice-mail). Doing this reassures the caller that you will pass on the message. Avoid saying: "I will have him call you as soon as possible." It is not a good idea because you might not have a chance to tell him. Or he/she might not want to call this person back—perhaps he/she has more important clients waiting. It is better just to let the caller know that you will pass the message on. Say something like this:

> ❖ I will make sure he gets this message.
> ❖ I'll pass your message on to her as soon as I see her.
> ❖ I'll see that she gets the message as soon as she's back in the office.

5. Leaving voice mail messages

When leaving a voice mail message, follow these steps:

> ❖ Greet.
> ❖ Identify the person you would like to speak to.
> ❖ Identify yourself and possibly your organization.
> ❖ Explain the reason for your call.
> ❖ Highlight the action that you would like the receiver to follow (if any), or highlight what your action will be.
> ❖ Leave contact details if necessary.

Some examples are as follows:

> ❖ Hello, Sue. It's me, Lily calling from ABC High-tech Company. I was just calling to inform you that I would like to reschedule the meeting for next week. Is it possible to arrange it next Tuesday morning, as I have an urgent meeting in the afternoon? Please call me back on 278306758 when you have time. Thanks.
> ❖ Good morning. I am looking for Mr. Xiao Rong. This is Roger Dong from JCW Ltd. I would like to update you on the status of the project and believe that it is worth arranging a meeting. I will call you back tomorrow as I will be in meetings for the rest of the day. I will talk to you then. Thanks.

In order to make your voice-mail sound professional, please remember that you have to:

● **Prepare beforehand**

It is always a good idea to plan your message before picking up the phone. Think about the purpose of your call, and try to narrow it down to one or two concise sentences.

● **Keep your voice-mail message short and sweet**

If your message is long and rambling, the person you are trying to reach will not feel too

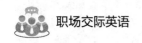

compelled to return your call. Try to keep your message between 20 to 30 seconds.

- **Speak clearly and slowly when leaving a voice-mail**

With a time limit of the call, you might feel pressured to fit as many words as possible into your message. If you are someone who tends to speak quickly, be mindful of that tendency when leaving messages. Focus on making every word clear and easy to understand. This is especially important if you are leaving a callback number.

- **Speak in your normal tone of voice**

Stick to your normal tone of voice. It will sound more genuine, more articulate, and people will be more likely to return your voice-mail.

- **Don't forget to introduce yourself**

Start every voice-mail message with a short introduction that includes your full name and company name.

- **Set clear expectations in your voice-mail**

Before you hang up the phone, your caller should understand what you want and why you are calling. In this way, the expectations are clear and there's no confusion about the next steps. With any luck, you will receive a call back in no time.

6. Call closure

If you are in a rush or if the conversation is rambling on, you have to end the call. To make it, simply refocus the conversation to the original point, give a reason for ending the call, and then wish them a great day. Try your best to keep a friendly tone when ending the conversation so that the call finishes on a positive note.

Ending an informal call politely

- **Refocus the conversation to the original point**

Phone calls often drag on because the conversation goes off track. Bring the call back to its original intention to quickly achieve the goal of the conversation so that you can end the call. If the goal of the conversation has already been met, simply say that you're glad you've achieved your objective. For instance:

❖ I'm so glad we've finally managed to fix a time to play tennis.

- **Summarize the call to signal that the conversation is winding down**

This is particularly useful if the call has diverged from the original point or if it has been a complex conversation. For example:

112

> ❖ It's been great to finally make a plan for our family holiday. To confirm the details, we are all meeting at Dad's house on Friday next week and will be coming back on Sunday.

If you want to summarize a casual conversation that didn't have an original point, say something like:

> ❖ It's been really nice hearing about your promotion. I'm really glad that your job is going well.

- **Make an excuse to finish the conversation quickly**

If the person you are talking to is rambling, consider making an excuse to quickly end the call. Try to be honest if possible, as this prevents you from ending up in a web of lies. For instance:

> ❖ My phone battery is getting low so I'd better go.
> ❖ I've got someone coming over shortly so I need to go.
> ❖ I'd better go to organize the kids.

Avoid using a long, elaborate excuse, as these tend to sound fake. Stick with a short, simple reason for leaving and then end the call.

- **Wrap up the call with a plan to talk again soon**

This is a polite way to signal that the conversation is coming to an end. Simply mention when you'll see the person next or say that it'd be great to catch up in-person soon. For instance:

> ❖ It's been lovely chatting. I'm looking forward to seeing you at school next week.
> ❖ It's been great catching up. Let's do it again soon.

- **Wish the caller a great day to signal the end of the conversation**

This is often used as a social cue to indicate that the call is about to end. Thank the caller for their time and then wish them the best. If they've already wished you the best, simply say "Thanks, you too." You can end a call with:

> ❖ It's been so nice talking with you. Have a great rest of your day!

If you have been talking about a specific topic during the call, wish them the best with it, if relevant. For example:

> ❖ So nice to catch up with you. All the best with your wedding planning.

- **Tell the caller that you won't keep them any longer as a polite exit**

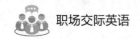

This is a great line to use as it doesn't place the blame for the long conversation on the caller. Instead, it infers that you do not want to hold them up on the phone. This is a good way to quickly end a call. When a natural lull in conversation occurs, say something like:

> ❖ Anyway, I'll let you go I don't want to hold you up any longer.
> ❖ I know how busy you are, so I won't keep chatting.

This is a useful option if you've already tried more subtle ways to end the conversation with no success. If they respond saying that you aren't keeping them from anything, politely say that you need to go.

Closing a business call professionally

• Ask the caller if there is anything else you can help them with. This helps to focus on the conversation. Ask the caller if you have addressed their concern and if they have any more questions or queries. If they want further information, simply address the topic and then repeat the same question in order to close the call. Avoid saying "Is that all?", as this can come across as rude. It is best to ask if they need any more information or if they require any further help. If the other person is helping you, simply say that you are grateful for their help and end the call.

> ❖ Is there anything else I can help with before I go?

• Wait for a lull in the conversation to wrap things up. If you are not sure when to end the call, use the lull as an opportunity to do so. This makes the end of the conversation feel nice and natural. It works particularly well after asking if you can help the customer further. Once they say no, wait a few seconds to create a lull and then take the opportunity to bring the call to a close. If possible, avoid interrupting the caller, as this can come across rudely.

• Give a polite reason for ending the call. If the call has gotten off topic or is no longer serving a useful purpose, use a natural lull in conversation to say that you need to go. Try to be as polite and honest as possible, as this comes across more professional than a poor excuse. For instance:

> ❖ I've got a meeting in 10 minutes so I better go.
> ❖ It was a pleasure talking with you about your feedback. I just noticed that my call queue is starting to stack up, though—is there anything else I can help with before I go?
> ❖ A client has just arrived that I need to speak with.

• Thank the person for their call to signal the end of the conversation. If necessary, thank the caller for any advice they gave and for any actions they've committed to. If you can't think of anything specific to thank them for, simply tell them that you appreciate the time they have taken to talk to you. For instance:

> ❖ Thanks for your time today—I really appreciate it.
> ❖ It's been really useful hearing about your new customer service system.

● Wish the caller the best and say goodbye. It is best to use this technique after you have wrapped up the call, as it can seem a little rude if you quickly say goodbye mid-conversation. Take the time to say why you need to go, thank them for their time, and then wish them a good day. For instance:

> ❖ Thanks for your time today. Have a wonderful rest of your day. Speak soon.

Try to maintain a polite and friendly tone when ending a conversation. This helps the call to end on a positive note. If you have a limited amount of time to talk, try to mention this at the beginning of the call to warn the person in advance.

 Practice and activity

1. Think about what you would say in these situations.

EXAMPLE: You are the boss of a restaurant. The phone rings and you pick it up, the caller asks "Is it Sam's Restaurant?" What do you say?

Yes, Sam's, Feng's speaking.

a. Your female colleague just gave birth to a baby and takes a paternity leave. What do you say to the caller who wants to speak to her?

_____

b. You are Present Zhang's assistant and he is on a business trip and there is a call for him. What do you say to the caller?

_____

c. Leave a voice-mail to your colleague Fang Fang and ask her to call you back when she gets the message.

_____

d. You did not catch the caller's name and the phone number he gave. You are not sure whether the number ends with fourteen or forty. Ask him to repeat.

_____

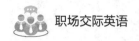

2. Case study

Please read the case and work in groups to figure out the inappropriateness.

> Mary was going on a vacation, and wouldn't be in her office for several days. She changed her office voice-mail too. "You've reached Mary Ma at ABC High-tech Company, I'll be unavailable between July 8th and July 14th. Leave your name, number, and reason for calling and I'll get back to you. If it's an emergency, call my colleague Peter Wu at extension 888."
>
> On her return she had several voice-mails to return. She reached everyone who had called her with the exception of Bill Johnson. She left a message with Bill's voice-mail, saying, "Good afternoon, this is Mary Ma with ABC High-tech Company returning your call. I'm back at the office, and you can reach me at my regular hours. Have a good evening."

Section 3   Telephoning strategies

Understanding others on the telephone can be difficult. Misunderstandings can happen easily, partly because we can't see the speaker's body language, facial expressions or lip movements. You can avoid miscommunication by using various strategies. For instance:

- **Know what you are going to say**

Have an outline with a few bullet points about your main reason for calling or for having this conversation. It's important to prepare your content for the telephone call if you are the one placing the call. Also, include the following bits of information:

> ➤ **Why are you calling?** (For example, are you calling for information about something, Are you placing a food order? Is it a business call? Are you making a doctor's appointment or another one like at a hair salon? Are you calling the bank?)
>
> ➤ **Who are you speaking with/Who is your audience? Do you know this person?**
>
> ➤ **What is the purpose of the call?** (to schedule an appointment, to catch up with a friend, to order food, etc.)

If you are the person receiving the phone call, it's a good idea to jot down a few notes or bullet points as you listen to the person introduce themselves and figure out why they are calling. You can always follow up with another call or even an email if you need some time to think about what they said or what they are asking.

- **Slow it down**

The phone is a lower resolution communication channel, meaning we only hear the person's voice, we can't see them. For this reason, it's important to speak slower than you would if you were in a face-to-face conversation. Speak as clearly as possible and enunciate your words. Since you are speaking a bit more slowly, you also buy yourself some thinking time. Meaning, you can think about what you are going to say before saying it. Also, it gives the other person an opportunity to ask questions if they missed something.

- **Do a comprehension check**

If you are giving someone information, have them repeat it to you. The easiest example of this is when you give a phone number or address. Make sure they have understood it and recorded it correctly. You can ask them to repeat the number back to you or spell out the address or email to ensure they got it. You can say:

> ❖ Would you please read that back to me?
> ❖ Would you please repeat the phone number so I know you got it?
> ❖ Could you say that again?

The caller can use a spelling alphabet (using words that stand for specific letters) to ensure that the person who takes the message on the other side of the phone gets the name correctly. For instance:

> ❖ My last name is Kate. That's K as in key, A as in apple, T as in tree, E as in egg.

- **Get confirmation**

Similar to doing a comprehension check, you also want to make sure that you've understood the information correctly. You can say, for instance:

> ❖ So to confirm, we're meeting on the 21st at noon at the comer cafe?
> ❖ So the school is on Hope St.? Is that correct?
> ❖ So, your number is 888-235-7850?

That ensures you're both on the same page. This could also be an opportunity to get clarification.

- **Use your non-verbal forms of communication**

With phone calls, even when we can't see the person or they can't see us, non-verbal communication is still important, which includes our hand gestures, facial expressions, and micro-expressions—those quick expressions that flash across our faces within a fraction of a second. When we speak to someone in person, we are using our non-verbals. We use our hands when we talk naturally. Believe it or not, using your hand gestures on a phone call can help you express yourself and deliver your message clearly.

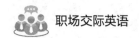

The above mentioned 5 ways can help have a successful telephone conversation in English. If you're placing the call, have an outline with points you will be making and questions you'll ask. If you are receiving the call, have a notepad handy so that you can jot down a few notes and questions you might have during the phone call. Use your hand gestures to help you articulate the message and speak more confidently. You can slow down your speech so that you have time to think and ask/answer questions. Check their comprehension to make sure you're on the same page. And as the receiver of information, you can also get confirmation and even clarification in some cases.

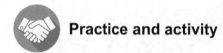

Practice and activity

Prepare and role-play with a partner a dialogue for the following scenario.

❖ **Student A**

You have a job interview at ABC High-tech Company. The secretary will call you to give you information about the date, time and location of the interview. He/she will also tell you the names of the people who will interview you.

- *Take down the information*
- *Use any of the strategies above to clarify information you do not understand*

❖ **Student B**

You are the secretary at ABC High-tech Company. Call your partner to invite him/her to a job interview on October 18 at 2:15 p.m. at your headquarters in Shenzhen. The interviewers are Wenzhou Cen, Shouhua Lee and Dafeng Zhang.

- *Begin your call with a professional greeting*
- *Clarify information your partner does not understand*
- *End the call appropriately*

References

ADVANCED ENGLISH. How to Have a Successful Telephone Conversation in English [EB/OL]. 2013-08-18. https://advancedenglish.co/blog/zausans5/how-to-have-a-successful-telephone-conversation-in-english.

AMARESAN S. The 11 Essential Rules of Phone Etiquette [EB/OL]. 2020-07-23. https://blog.hubspot.com/service/phone-etiquette.

Contact Center World [EB/OL]. [2013-08-18]. https://www.contactcenterworld.com/company/blog/conversational/?id=a4445dd8-c0a3-4566-83ee-9baaffc32661.

JOSEPH C. Steps of Making a Business Telephone Call [EB/OL]. 2013-08-18. https://smallbusiness.chron.com/steps-making-business-telephone-call-218.html.

MCCUTCHEOM M. https://blog.hubspot.com/service/phone-etiquette [EB/OL]. 2023-03-16. https://www.wikihow.com/Make-Effective-Business-Phone-Calls#Preparing-for-a-Call.

MCGRAW HILL. Telephone Communication [EB/OL]. 2013-08-18. https://www. mheducation. es/bcv/guide/capitulo/8448180860.pdf.

SETTLEMENT AT WORK. Telephone Strategies [EB/OL]. 2013-08-18. https://www. settlementatwork.org/lincdocs/linc5-7/telephone.calls/pdfs/telephone.LINC6/06.telephone.str ategies.pdf.

SWEENEY G. Phone Etiquette at Work: How to Answer Calls Professionally [EB/OL]. 2019-09-08. https://telzio.com/blog/phone-etiquette.

WORKPLACE ENGLISH TRAINING. Introduction [EB/OL]. 2013-08-18. https:// www.workplace-english-training.com/elibrary/en/.

Chapter 9

Business meetings

Meetings are an important part of the modern workplace and individuals need to develop effective communication skills for them. Understanding the right phrases, language and conversational tone to use during a workplace meeting will help with career progression in our fast-paced international trade.

 Learning Objectives

➤ Understand the basic procedures of running workplace meetings
➤ Know the basic English expressions used on workplace meetings
➤ Perform appropriately and politely on workplace meetings

Section 1　Basics of business meetings

There are various kinds of meetings, such as information-giving meeting, routine meeting, decision-making meeting. Although there seem to be quite different methods of analyzing a meeting, in practice there is a tendency for certain kinds of meetings to sort themselves out into one of three categories.

● **Daily meeting**

People work together on the same project with a common objective and reach decisions informally by general agreement.

● **Weekly or monthly meeting**

Members work on different but parallel projects, and there is a certain competitive element and a greater likelihood that the chairman will make the final decision himself.

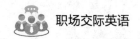

- **The irregular, occasional, or "special project" meeting**

People whose normal work does not bring them into contact or has little or no relationship to the others are united only by the project. Thus the meeting exists to promote and they are motivated by the desire that the project should succeed. Though actual voting is uncommon, every member effectively has a veto.

No matter what kind of meeting it is and regardless of the objective, it is important for every person in the work place to know how to run a meeting.

1. Running a meeting

In an earlier University of North Carolina study, researchers found a link between how workers feel about the effectiveness of meetings and their job satisfaction. Thus, it is important to know how to run meetings effectively and efficiently. The following procedures can help make the time colleagues and employees spend together more meaningful.

- **Prior to the meeting**
  - ➢ Plan. Think about questions such as "Why are we meeting?", "Who should attend the meeting?", "What is the desired outcome?", "How can we achieve that?".
  - ➢ Make arrangements for the meeting, i.e. arranging for guest speakers, hospitality, venue, date and time.
  - ➢ Write an agenda that is detailed enough to allow all those attending the meeting to arrive fully informed and prepared.
  - ➢ Send adequate notice of the meeting to all concerned.
  - ➢ Minutes of the previous meeting should be enclosed if they have not already been sent.

- **At the meeting**

Meeting procedures may vary according to the level of formality required to complete the agenda efficiently. Usually there is a chairperson who presides over the event to ensure that participants are following the conventions of the meeting. The chairperson usually has to complete the following tasks:

- ➢ Open a meeting by greeting everyone and introducing him/herself.
- ➢ Start the actual meeting by stating objectives and introducing the agenda and sticking to the item on the agenda.
- ➢ Prevent interruptions and keep discussion on track.
- ➢ Get through the business on time.

> Involve everyone in the meeting.

> Summarize discussion and actions to be taken.

> Close meetings.

As the participants of the meeting, their roles include:

> Undertake any necessary preparation prior to the meeting.

> Arrive on time.

> Listen to the opinions of others.

> Participate.

> Ask questions to clarify understanding.

> Avoid side conversations that distract others.

● **After the meeting**

The follow-up is also important at a meeting. It ensures that everything is done and has been discussed during the meeting. Usually, the following actions have to be taken after the meeting:

> Write minutes as soon as possible.

> Write follow up e-mails.

> Allow time to talk to new people.

> Talk to your committee members about how the meeting went.

> Follow up with any action agreed during the meeting.

> Start thinking about the next meeting.

Section 2   English phrases for a workplace meeting

Understanding the right phrases, language and conversational tone to use during a workplace meeting will help with career progression in the fast-paced international economy. In this section, widely used phrases by the chairperson and participants are introduced.

1. Chairperson

● **Leading a meeting in English**

When leading a meeting, it's important that the chairperson welcomes everyone and asks everyone to introduce themselves and provide a brief meeting agenda. A formal business meeting could start in the following ways:

> Welcoming and introducing the participants.

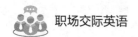

You can start with a simple greeting, using phrases such as:

❖ Good morning, everyone. If we're all here, let's get started.
❖ Hello, everyone. Thank you for coming today.
❖ Welcome, everybody. Thank you for coming.
❖ I'd like to welcome everyone.
❖ I'd like to thank everyone for coming today.
❖ We are pleased to welcome everyone.
❖ After greeting them, introduce yourself.
❖ I'm (your name). I'll keep this meeting brief as I know you're all busy people.
❖ I'm (your name) and I arranged this meeting because...

➢ Asking others to introduce themselves.

It is essential that individuals attending the meeting are well-acquainted with each other. If the participants do not know each other, the person leading the meeting could ask everyone to introduce themselves in the following ways:

❖ Let's go around the table and introduce ourselves, (your name) do you want to start?
❖ Let's introduce ourselves quickly, please state your name, job title and why you are here?

➢ Setting the agenda and outlining the objectives.

It is essential to start the meeting by outlining the agenda clearly and the key objectives of the meeting. The objectives can be stated with the following phrases:

❖ There are (number) items on the agenda. First...
❖ Today I would like to outline our plans for...
❖ Shall we take the points in this order?
❖ OK, as you can see from the agenda...there are (number) items.
❖ Firstly,... secondly, ... thirdly, ... and finally,...
❖ Let's start by talking about..., then go onto..., and finish with...
❖ I've called this meeting in order to...
❖ We're here today to discuss...
❖ Our aim/objective is to.../The goal of today's meeting is to...

➢ Controlling the meeting.

As a chair, you should work through the sections on the agenda, making sure people stick to the point, and that there are enough contributions for decisions to be made or action to be taken. The following phrases can be used for various purposes.

● **Moving forward**

The following phrases are for the transition to the main focus of the meeting.

> ❖ So, if there is nothing else we need to discuss, let's move on to today's agenda.
> ❖ Shall we get down to business?
> ❖ Is there any other business?
> ❖ If there are no further developments, I'd like to move on to today's topic.
> ❖ Once again, I'd like to thank you all for coming. Now, shall we get down to business?

● Timing/Duration

It is often a good idea to inform all participants the timing of meeting in advance. Phrases used are as follows:

> ❖ I would like to wrap-up by (time) o'clock.
> ❖ The meeting is scheduled to finish at (time) o'clock, and I'd like to finish on time.
> ❖ We're pretty short of time, so could you please be brief?
> ❖ Can we keep each item to about (number) minutes?

● Allocating the roles

As the meeting is moved through, it is important that people keep track of what's going on.

> ❖ (name of participant) has agreed to take the minutes
> ❖ (name of participant) has kindly agreed to give us a report on this matter.
> ❖ (name of participant) will lead point 1, (name of participant) point 2, and (name of participant) point 3.
> ❖ (name of participant), would you mind taking notes today?
> ❖ We will hear a short report on each point first, followed by a discussion round the table.
> ❖ We'll have to keep each item to ten minutes. Otherwise we'll never get through.
> ❖ We may need to vote on item (number), if we can't get a unanimous decision.

● Inviting opinions

Chairperson needs to get all participants involved in the meeting. The phrases used for inviting opinions are as follows:

> ❖ What do you all think?
> ❖ What are everyone's thoughts on this? Does anyone have an opinion on this topic?
> ❖ I'd like to give the floor to...
> ❖ Does anyone have anything else to add?
> ❖ What are your views on this?

● Moving on to a different point

In order to give every item on the agenda a full discussion, the chairperson has to move on to different points:

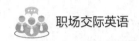

❖ Could we move on to item 2 on the agenda?

❖ If nobody has anything else to add, perhaps we could look at the next point/let's move on to the next item.

❖ I think we've spent enough time on this topic, let's move on...

❖ We're running short on time, so let's move on.

❖ Can we move on to the next point before it gets too late?

Keeping/sticking to the agenda

It is the chairman's responsibility to keep the meeting on track. If you find that the discussion is going off the topic, you can bring the discussion back on topic by using these phrases:

❖ I think we're digressing.

❖ Can we get back on topic?

❖ Let's get back on track, OK?

❖ I think we are getting a bit off topic.

❖ I'm afraid that's outside the scope of this meeting.

❖ We're getting a little side tracked.

● Reminding the meeting length

It is quite common in a meeting that people talk much longer than scheduled. In that case, you can use these phrases to remind them:

❖ We're getting pretty short of time.

❖ We've spent 15 minutes on this already. Let's move on to something else.

❖ We're running out of time.

❖ OK, everyone, we're almost out of time. We're getting really behind schedule.

● Handling interruptions

As a chairperson or a presenter, you have to know different ways of handling interruptions. For instance, you can promise to come back to a point later, politely disagree with an interruption, or say the interruption is not relevant or that time is short, politely accept the interruption and respond to it before continuing. These are the phrases that could be used:

❖ Yes, go ahead.

❖ Sorry, please let me finish...

❖ If I may finish this point...

❖ Can I come to that later?

❖ That's not really relevant at this stage...

❖ Can we leave that to another discussion?

❖ I'm afraid I can't agree with you on that. As I was saying…

❖ That's out of the question.

- **Closing and scheduling the next meeting**

At the end of the meeting, the chairperson has to summarize the meeting and bring it to an end and set a time for the next meeting. The following phrases are used:

> ❖ We have to bring this to a close.
> ❖ I think we have covered everything we'd planned to. I don't think there's anything else left.
> ❖ If no one has anything else to add, then I think we'll wrap this up.
> ❖ OK. Let's finish there. Thank you all for coming and I'll see you again in the next week.
> ❖ Let's call it a day.
> ❖ That will be all for today.
> ❖ I think we should end there. Just to summarize...
> ❖ We've covered everything, so I'd like to go over the decisions we've taken...
> ❖ So, to conclude...we've agreed...
> ❖ I'd just like to summarize the key points.
> ❖ So, to summarize...
> ❖ We will meet again (date)...
> ❖ Let's set a time for our next meeting.

2. Participants

Active participation in the meeting is reflected by asking questions and interrupting the presenter politely if you do not understand what is being said, or if there is agreement/disagreement. It is a good idea to show that you are actively involved in the meeting.

- **Interrupt politely**

If you accidentally speak over someone or have something to add to what is being said, you can interrupt with the following phrases:

> ❖ Sorry, but just to clarify.
> ❖ Sorry I didn't quite hear that, can you say it again?
> ❖ That's an excellent point (person's name), what about doing (action point) as well?
> ❖ From our departments perspective, it's a little more complicated. Let me explain.

You can also use phrases such as:

> ❖ Excuse me for interrupting.
> ❖ I've never thought about it that way before. How does it affect (this point)?

- **Asking questions**

There are many different ways to ask questions during the meeting. The following phrases are suitable when asking for someone to repeat what they have said:

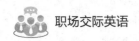

❖ I'm sorry, I missed that. Could you repeat that, please?

❖ I'm not sure I follow. Could you go over that point again, please?

❖ Can you repeat that please?

❖ Can you run that by me one more time?

❖ Can you repeat that in a simplified way?

For clarification the following phrases should be used:

❖ I don't fully understand what you mean. Could you explain it from a different angle?

❖ Could you explain to me how that is going to work?

❖ Just to be clear, do you mean this (repeat the explained point in the way you understand it)?

For more information, the following phrases should be used:

❖ Could you say a little more about that, please?

❖ Would you elaborate on that a little?

❖ Could you go into a little more detail about...?

❖ Can you give an example of what you're saying?

- **Agreeing and disagreeing**

There are many levels of agreement:

disagree totally   wait to be convinced   limited agreement   agreement but no conviction   committed totally

Here are the phrases for agreeing and disagreeing

➢ **Total disagreement**

❖ I totally disagree.

❖ I couldn't agree less.

❖ You must be joking!

➢ **Wait to be convinced**

❖ I can see what you're getting at.

❖ There are two sides to the argument.

❖ On the one hand...on the other hand...

❖ I'm not sure/convinced about,...

❖ I just think we need more time.

> **Limited agreement**

❖ I agree, but...
❖ I'm not against it, but...
❖ Yes, I'm with you.

Section 3   Rules of a good meeting

Bad meetings are typically the result of a lack of a focus, agenda, or structure. And one of the best tools you can use to make sure you stay productive is agreeing on a set of meeting rules, which are the standards or guidelines set up ahead of time that the meeting attendees should follow for the meeting to be as productive and successive as possible. Here are the basic rules:

- **Come prepared**

This could look differently depending on the type of meeting and each individual's role within the meeting. In general, your team should:

> Read the meeting agenda beforehand.

> Come ready with talking points or potential questions.

> Consider what questions they may be asked, so they can be ready with answers.

> Be ready to contribute an update on their responsibilities or tasks.

- **Show up on time**

A timely meeting is an effective meeting, and starting as planned is an important meeting rule. This sets the correct example for how things should be done across the company and shows that you as the organizer value team members' time. What's more, a meeting that starts on time is more likely to end on time. The agenda should outline and estimate how much time each point will take. When beginning the meetings, the organizer or chair should present the agenda so all participants get a chance to align on upcoming topics and a refresh of major topics.

- **Follow the agenda**

No matter if it's a daily stand-up or quarterly board meeting, the basic rule that every meeting should have is to follow the agenda. Having this expectation in place ensures that the conversations stay on track, all necessary talking points are discussed, and that all voices are heard. It's also a great way to ensure that the meeting doesn't exceed its scheduled time and run too long.

- **Stay within the time scheduled for the meeting**

Losing track of time is easy to do, especially if a meeting is covering interesting and

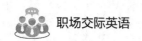
important topics (as always occurs). Unfortunately, a poorly timed meeting is not very effective since it can cut into participants' other commitments, hold them back from hitting daily goals in their work, and lead to agitation. As the organizer, it is your responsibility to stay with the time, and you have to feel free to interject at an appropriate moment to bring a topic to a close or move onto the next one.

- **Create an inclusive environment**

The meeting needs to be an inclusive space for everyone attending so that it can be deemed as successful with a productive and thought-provoking conversation. To accomplish this, the organizer or chairperson has to make time for everyone to speak and participate and be patient and not interrupt others. Besides, he/she has to respect each other's thoughts or opinions and value everyone's different inputs, and remain open to new ideas and embrace different communication styles.

- **Record action items and decisions**

It can be difficult to remember each action item, decision, or question that was communicated in a meeting. Because of this, it's crucial that these are recorded as the meeting progresses. Meeting minutes will always come in handy if you need to circle back on a point, where you are missing evidence of a decided-upon deadline, or need to remember who was assigned which task.

- **Create precise tasks and deadlines**

You should always aim to close the critical topics of every meeting. This involves making clear deadlines with clear deadlines so that all relevant participants know their next steps.

 Practice and activity

1. Explain the function of each meeting phrase. The first one is done for you as an example.

a. We need to finish at/by 11 o'clock.	*Timing*
b. Good morning, everyone.	
c. I've called this meeting in order to…	
d. We will adjourn for lunch at 12.	
e. If we are all here, let's get started.	
f. Charlie has agreed to take the minutes.	
g. If nobody has anything to add, shall we leave that item?	
h. Pardon me. I'm not sure I understood you.	

2. Role-play: Choose one of the situations below (either from the list or by taking a card). Act out the situation with the help of your partner(s). Try to solve the problem by using suitable language for chairing a meeting.

(1) Participants will not stop chatting.

(2) No one at the meeting will continue to discuss.

(3) One person is dominating the conversation.

(4) Some one keeps interrupting.

(5) Participants take too much time discussing the agenda.

3. Discussion: The 20th National Congress of the Communist Party of China (CPC) on Oct. 22 approved the report presented by Xi Jinping on behalf of the 19th CPC Central Committee. Read the excerpt from the Report and answer the following questions.

"Employment is the most basic component of the people's well-being. We need to intensify efforts to implement the employment-first policy and improve related mechanisms to promote high-quality and full employment."

Instructions: You are the head of HR department in your company. The CEO of your company asks you to report how to answer the call of implementing the employment-first strategy. You want to know the thoughts of the department staff at first. Please hold a meeting to discuss the situation and decide which steps should be taken.

 ## References

BARNARD D. Common Business English Phrases for a Workplace Meeting [EB/OL]. 2018-02-17. https://virtualspeech.com/blog/english-phrases-workplace-meeting.

BEARE K. Useful English Phrases for Running a Business Meeting [EB/OL]. 2018-01-01. https://www.thoughtco.com/phrases-for-running-a-business-meeting-1209021.

CALVELLO M. 11 Meeting Rules For a Successful Meeting [EB/OL]. 2021-06-14. https://fellow.app/blog/meetings/meeting-ground-rules/.

JAY A. How to Run a Meeting [EB/OL]. 2023-08-18. https://hbr.org/1976/03/how-to-run- a-meeting.

USING ENGLISH. Chairing Meetings Problem Roleplays [EB/OL]. 2023-08-18. https://www. usingenglish.com/files/pdf/business-english-chairing-meetings-roleplay.pdf.

Chapter 10

Workplace communication etiquette and office culture

Communication etiquette in the workplace is very important. Whether you are writing to staff, talking to customers or negotiating with co-workers, it is very critical, because it creates a professional, mutually respectful environment that helps everyone in the office or at the workplace to communicate effectively and increase the organization's productivity. There are certain actions and behaviors you just shouldn't bring with you into a professional workplace. Doing so can have major negative impacts on your career. In this chapter, we will equip you with basic etiquette rules that ensure effective communication in the office or at workplace.

 Learning Objectives

➢ Understand the basic communication rules at workplace
➢ Know basic etiquette at workplace
➢ Communicate appropriately in the workplace with diverse cultural background

Section 1   Basic rules for communication at workplace

Rule No.1 Use the correct medium

There are many different ways to communicate in the workplace, and there are business etiquette rules for each medium. Some examples of different mediums include: e-mail, telephone, video conferencing tools like Tencent Meeting, instant messaging platforms like

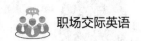

WeChat etc. Be sure to select the medium that best suits your message. For example, if you're looking to send a long memo about a project update, instant messaging is likely not a good choice. That kind of message is better sent through an e-mail. Similarly, don't select social media as the medium to discuss a critical business issue with a manager. That medium is better for personal matters. If you want to meet with a customer in person, it is best to call ahead and set up a meeting rather than showing up at his office unannounced. In most office etiquette guidelines, it is better to give the customer notice about your visit so as not to disrupt his day.

Rule No. 2 Keep it professional while being personable

Communication etiquette in the workplace requires that all conversation, whether written or verbal, should be professional. This means that proper grammar, sentence structure and punctuation should always be used in e-mails, instant messages and other written forms of communication. Use the correct e-mail thread when responding to a chain and be sure to keep the content succinct and clear.

Rule No. 3 Start with a greeting or seek permission

Start instant messaging with a greeting like "Hi" or "Hello". Also, be mindful of the good time to initiate the conversation by asking whether they would have a minute to help/answer you. Your message may be like "Hi, Mary, would you take a minute to sign the notice?". If the receiver can't help you at that moment, you can ask him the right time to chat.

Rule No. 4 Value other people's time and keep the conversations short

Stay focused on the topic by having a brief and clear conversation. Make your conversation productive by holding on to the subject of the conversation alone. If the recipient may take some time to respond to you, then you can choose the other medium of communication such as e-mail, or face to face meeting.

Rule No. 5 Be friendly & polite

Being professional or formal and being free from discriminatory language or swearing. Say "Thank You", "Please" to your colleagues. Chat in a polite way. Pay respect to the sender's chat by sending a short message such as "Yes", "Looking for it", "Checking now", etc. Avoid pointing out the typing errors of your sender or friends.

Rule No. 6 Abbreviate only when needed

Reduce the usage of abbreviations, acronyms, and slang. Adjust the type of communication when you chat with colleagues, higher officials or friends. Try to be clear with your words. Also, it is important to check the grammar before you send the message.

Rule No. 7 Use the correct body language

It is best to keep neutral body language in the workplace. Limit facial expressions and gestures. Avoid touching. Respect personal space. Do not get too close to others. Remember that body language varies between cultures. Even in the same workplace, people from different cultures may interpret body language in different ways. It is best to start with a neutral stance. Then, observe your coworkers and adjust your style accordingly.

Section 2   Workplace etiquette

When it comes to working in an office or other professional setting, etiquette matters. How you present yourself and interact with those around you can directly influence the trajectory of your career. The dos and don'ts as follows can help you behave appropriately at the workplace.

- **The don'ts**
- ➢ **Don't gossip about fellow coworkers or your boss.**

Gossiping is one of the cardinal sins of office work: Whether you're tempted to gossip about your boss, co-worker, or the company as a whole, you're not hurting anyone but yourself when you do. Gossiping can portray you as someone who can't be trusted or someone who isn't a team player, which won't help you reach your professional goals. It can also be duly harmful if it gets back to the target of the gossip.

➢ **Don't bring your emotions into the office.**

It is best to leave your personal emotions at the door when you get to work. Your desk neighbor does not want to hear your sob story from over the weekend. If you truly cannot focus on your work because something has happened, it is probably a better idea to take some personal time to process your emotions. Or, if something in the workplace is bothering you, reach out to the human resources department or your supervisor to resolve the issue so it does not interfere with your work.

➢ **Don't have personal conversations at your desk.**

If you must have a private or personal phone conversation when you're at work, try not to have the conversation at your desk where others can hear you. Many workplaces have conference rooms that you can use for phone calls; otherwise, it might be a good idea to step outside.

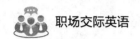

➤ **Don't talk back to your boss.**

You should never talk back to them. Always show your boss respect, and do your part not to be sarcastic or glib. This is not to say you can't disagree with them about aspects of the job, a project, or the company's strategy. You should always feel free to share thoughts or concerns if you've got them, but the way that you do it really matters.

● **The dos**

➤ **Do be on time.**

Punctuality is key! Don't be the one that everyone is waiting for to start the meeting. The most professional people often arrive at work first and leave last. Many employers are taking advantage of 24/7 communication to try to get the workers to put in hours late at night and on weekends. You may not get noticed for this work, but you will get noticed for showing up early and not having your coat on or laptop packed at 4:55 pm each evening. Arrive five or more minutes earlier. When you have assignments, submit them as early as possible rather than at the last minute.

➤ **Do dress appropriately in the office.**

What constitutes appropriate will depend on the particular culture of your workplace. But it's always a good idea to dress to impress, especially when you're first starting a new role at a company. Even if you don't have a formal dress code, save the crop tops, flip-flops, and see-through shirts for the weekend. Surely, no one will take you seriously if you don't.

➤ **Do take care of your pitch and tone at the workplace.**

Never shout at anyone or use foul words. It is unprofessional to lash out at others under pressure. Stay calm and think rationally.

➤ **Do stay current with technology.**

Whether or not you feel you need to use a particular social media tool or smart phone app, if many others in your circle are using it, learn it. You might not want to tweet, but it's a good idea to know what Twitter is about so you won't sound out of touch in group discussions. Not having a WeChat or QQ might make you seem unsociable or behind the times. Embrace new technology to let others know you stay abreast of the rapidly changing business environment. Listen to what your peers are talking about and note what technology they are using to stay relevant and part of the conversation.

Section 3   Work culture around the world

The following article introduced work culture around the world. Read in detail to know the cultural differences.

- **On the clock around the world: International work culture**

Wake up. Clock in. Clock out. Sleep. Repeat. It's a familiar rhythm for the billions of people around the world who make up the global workforce. Though individual countries' work culture and habits differ, the concept of working to earn a living—however, begrudgingly—is one that most laborers and employees know well, no matter where they are in the world. Truth is, as much as people around the globe love to gripe and groan about it, work, whether we're making small talk by the water cooler or glued to a computer screen, is an essential part of our lives that lets us enjoy the personal time we get when we're not in the office.

That being said, the structure and nature of work take many forms across the planet, and of course it depends on what type of work you're doing; not everyone follows the same standards and rules across different industries, even within the same countries. Here's a look at some elements of work culture around the world.

- **Work, work, work culture**

When it comes to business, Americans certainly have a reputation for, well, getting down to business. For a country with an exorbitantly high GDP that churns out products and results across all types of industries—manufacturing, entertainment and finance, to name a few—this reputation is not unfounded. Maybe it's the capitalistic ethos that drives the nation's economic policy at home and on the world stage, or perhaps it's how much corporations are tied up with politics. Whatever it is, many Americans work under the assumption that time is money, having been culturally shaped to prioritize output—and the hustle. It's a "rise and grind" culture that has made the all-too-relatable millennial meme "let's get this bread" so popular among the younger members of the United States' workforce; it captures the idea that whether or not they want to get up and work in the morning, they've got to play the game to earn the dough.

Americans aren't the only ones around the world who are known to work hard. Japan has a solid reputation for a strong work ethic—and all the consequences that follow it. Working a lot is sewn into the fabric of Japanese society, due in no small part to the country's economic rebuilding efforts after World War II. It's not unheard of for some of the nation's people to work dozens, even more than a hundred hours of overtime each month, with 6- or

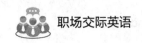

7-day workweeks and 12-hour days, putting in loads of work and strain on their bodies, minds and health.

All of this is not to say that Americans, the Japanese and other members of work-centric cultures don't know how to draw the line between personal and professional life. Barring the workaholics who are attached at the hip to their work emails, many busy bees in places like these love to relax and take time off to spend with family and friends, or to travel and see the world when they can squeeze out a few extra vacation days.

Be careful not to jump to the conclusion that the countries that work the most and the longest hours are also the most miserable. You might be surprised to learn that there are dozens of other nations that work longer days on average than Americans do—though their reputations might not represent this reality. According to the Organization for Economic Co-Operation and Development, Costa Rica takes the second-place title for the most hours worked yearly on average—and it's also often labeled one of the world's happiest countries. Other countries like Turkey, Mexico and the Republic of Korea, among others, round out the top of the list of most hours worked yearly on average, but that doesn't necessarily mean each country's work culture is as extreme or intense as in other parts of the world.

A better balance

A proper work-life balance is key to staying sane and stable in all aspects of one's life. But how countries treat this dynamic varies across the planet.

Jobs and work in some parts of the world are inextricably linked with personal identity. When you're talking with a stranger or a new friend, the question "What do you do?" might be totally appropriate in a place like the United States or Canada, but it's seen as more gauche or taboo if you're in Europe, where one's job isn't as interwoven with their livelihood. Many Europeans see jobs as just one fraction of a multidimensional life, and they'd rather not blather on about work if there's more interesting content to riff on.

You can get a sense of the work-life balance around the world by taking a look at how people from different countries value the time they spend not working—that is, how much vacation they typically take every year or the ways they're encouraged to squeeze the most out of their personal lives around their jobs when they're not working. As a part of a wave of labor reforms, France has the Right to Disconnect Law, which gives the country's citizens the right to ignore any work emails that arrive after business hours—an attempt to help the French people clearly establish a work-life balance.

Some countries really value giving laborers designated time to rest and relax. Whereas in the United States paid vacation time hovers around only 16 days a year on average (and even still, workers sometimes opt out of the time off they've earned because not showing up to work regularly is so stigmatized in American work culture), countries like Italy mandate that employees take at least 20 days of paid vacation a year (in addition to 10 national holidays), and England guarantees five weeks.

Parental leave is another big aspect of benefits in other countries. Over in Iceland, the government has instituted lenient parental leave policies that allow both parents of a newborn child to take three months each—at 80 percent of their salaries—and then split an extra three months of leave between them. Just a short hop across the Atlantic, the Scandinavian countries are renowned for their generous family leave policies (among a whole host of other social benefits). The Swedes get 480 days of paid time off when they give birth to babies or adopt children. These countries—and others like the Netherlands, France, Canada and Germany—work the fewest number of hours on average, according to the OECD.

On the clock

How employees and workers portion their time throughout the day offers insights into work culture around the world. For example, the Swedish fika, or coffee break, is a staple of the country's daily grind. Whether formalized at particular points throughout the work day—like at 9 or 10 in the morning and 3 in the afternoon—or a more casual, fluid get-together, fika is built on the Swedish idea that productivity is highest when employees have a chance to relax and let off some steam. The breaks are a time for light conversation and camaraderie with coworkers that is thought to build morale.

Similarly, you might have heard of the Spanish siesta and envied the world-famous midday nap that seems to be characteristic of Iberian culture. While it is true that Spaniards often take a descanso, or "break," in the mid-afternoon—often to run errands or take a long lunch—less than half of the country's working population actually uses the time to sleep. This work culture custom is more of a relic of Spain's history than it is a representation of the sleepy behavior of an entire country (and the afternoon break is not exclusive to Spain, either). On average, Spaniards don't work less time than their European counterparts; their days are just more spread out. Even still, the concept of a two-hour break to rest and recharge in the middle of the day is not likely to be one that would fly in a strict, straight-edged work culture.

The rules and standards around the value of time are similarly looser in a place like Italy, where punctuality is less essential than it is in, say, the United States. It's not outrageous in India to be 15 minutes late or in Brazil to be even a half-hour late to a gathering. And meetings in the Arab world tend to spend ample time on pleasantries and personal connection

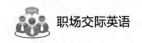
instead of jumping right into business, which can be seen as impolite. When it comes to deadlines, be cautious about setting them in South Africa, as the people in this country often view these project endpoints as more flexible suggestions rather than hard restrictions.

Knowing the norms and nuances of worldwide work culture can build your cultural competence on many levels. You might think that work is work anywhere you go, but getting a job abroad is a great immersion experiment that can open you up to brand new perspectives on living—while you're earning a living.

 ## References

AHMED A. Workplace Communication Etiquette [EB/OL]. 2019-04-29. https://bizfluent.com/info-8282891-workplace-communication-etiquette.html.

CHRISTINA Z. 6 Ways to Change Your Work Culture [EB/OL]. 2023-08-18. https://www.itagroup.com/insights/ways-to-change-your-work-culture.

DOOCHIN D. On the Clock Around the World: International Work Culture [EB/OL]. 2019-04-05. https://www.babbel.com/en/magazine/work-culture-around-the-world.

MALEDUCAT. Workplace Communication Etiquette 8 Rules: How To Do It Best [EB/OL]. 2021-07-16. https://mal-educat.com/workplace-communication/.

MILANO S. How to Become a More Professional Business Person [EB/OL]. 2017-07-05. https://careertrend.com/become-professional-business-person-10278.html.

MIND TOOLS CONTENT TEAM. Building Good Work Relationships [EB/OL]. 2023-08-18. https://www.mindtools.com/aorqe4z/building-good-work-relationships.